Vanillekipferln

210 g	Margarine
280 g	Mehl
100 g	Mandeln, samt Schale gerieben
30 g	Zucker

Alles zusammen mit dem Hand-
rührgerät gut verrühren, bis die
Masse weich ist. Kipferln formen.
Bei mäßiger Hitze backen (175° beim
Elektroherd), nicht braun werden
lassen. Heiß mit einer Mischung aus
Puder- und Vanillezucker bestreuen.

PRIMA PUBLISHING

PRIMA PUBLISHING and colophon are registered trademarks of Prima Communications, Inc.

Illustrations by Helene Stevens

Library of Congress Cataloging-in-Publication Data

Besser, Jeanne
    The first book of baking: more than 200 classic recipes and practical baking tips / by Jeanne Besser.
        p.   cm.
   Includes index.
   ISBN 0-7615-0727-2
   1. Baking. I. Title.
TX763.G567 1996
641.8'15—dc20   96-43286
                                              CIP

96 97 98 99 00 01 DD 10 9 8 7 6 5 4 3 2 1

Printed in the United States of America

How to Order
Single copies may be ordered from Prima Publishing, P.O. Box 1260BK, Rocklin, CA 95677; telephone (916) 632-4400. Quantity discounts are also available. On your letterhead, include information concerning the intended use of the books and the number of books you wish to purchase.

Visit us online at http://www.primapublishing.com

To Richard and Alexander, who sweeten my life.

Contents

❧ ❧

Acknowledgments   ix

Introduction   xi

Basics   1

Equipment   2

Ingredients   3

Before Baking   5

Measuring Ingredients   7

Baking   7

Keeping Clean   8

After Baking   9

Freezing   9

Presentation   10

Plate Decoration   10

Dessert Decoration   11

Muffins and Quick Breads   15

Date-Nut Bread   20

Lemon–Poppy Seed Muffins   22

Banana-Nut Muffins   24

Pumpkin Bread   26

Blueberry Muffins   28

Bran Muffins   30

Scones   32

Biscuits   34

Cranberry-Orange Bread   36

Popovers   38

Banana Bread   40

Zucchini Bread   42

Corn Muffins   44

Chocolate Chip Muffins   46

Cookies   47

Chocolate Biscotti   55

Blondies   58

Brownies   60

Butter Cookies   62

Gingersnaps   64

Toffee Bars   66

Chocolate Chip Cookies   68

Ranger Granger Cookies   70

Cream Cheese Brownies   72

Macaroons   74

Gingerbread People   76

Biscotti   79

Lace Cookies   82

Lemon Bars   84

Oatmeal Raisin Cookies   86

Chocolate–Chocolate Chip Cookies   88

Peanut Butter Cookies   90

Rice Crispy Marshmallow Bars   92

Shortbread   94

Sugar Christmas Cookies   96

Cakes   99

Boston Cream Pie   112

German Chocolate Cake   115

Lemon–Poppy Seed Cake   118

Carrot Cake with Cream Cheese Frosting   120

Yellow Layer Cake   122

Chocolate Layer Cake   124

Angel Food Cake   126

Sponge Cake   129

Pound Cake   132

Strawberry Shortcake   134

Coffee Cake   137

Cheesecake   140

Vanilla Frosting   144

Chocolate Frosting   146

Pies   147

Pie Crust   160

Cookie Crusts   162

Apple Pie   163

Peach Pie   166

Pumpkin Pie   168

Strawberry-Rhubarb Pie   170

Blueberry Pie   172

Chocolate Cream Pie   174

Lemon Meringue Pie   177

Banana Cream Pie   181

Fruit Cobbler   184

Key Lime Pie   186

Mud Pie   188

Cherry Pie   190

Fruit Crisp   192

Pecan Pie   194

Sweet Potato Pie   196

Breads   199

White Bread   211

Sourdough Bread   214

Whole Wheat Bread   218

Dinner Rolls   221

French Bread   224

Focaccia   227

Pecan Sticky Rolls   230

Cinnamon Rolls   233

Pizza Dough   236

Index   *239*

Acknowledgments

I'd like to thank Jennifer Basye Sander for her help in bringing this book to fruition, Debra Venzke for her help on the project, and Harris Golden for his time and expertise.

I'd like to thank Lynne Alpern, Esther Blumenfeld, David Groff, Jennifer Thompson, and Chuck Allen for their early guidance; Linda Martin, Jodi Long, Rosemary Rossi, Sarah François-Poncet, Lorraine Phillips, and Ken Zangwill for their encouragement and friendship; Jen Cosgrove, who took care of what was really important; and Susana Jones—every cookbook author needs an even better step instructor.

And most of all, thank you to my families, the Hobermans and the Bessers, for their love, support, and enthusiasm; and to Richard, Alexander, and Babe, who were constantly surrounded by flying flour, forced to eat a lot of desserts, and never complained.

Introduction

On a chilly February afternoon when I was fourteen, our beloved housekeeper, Minnie, enlisted my help in making a red cake for Valentine's Day. My curiosity was instantly aroused. I had seen boxes for devil's food cake and boxes for white cake, but never one for a red cake. What did she know that I didn't?

Instead of venturing to the cupboard for the cake mix as she normally did during our baking adventures, Minnie began pulling things out of our pantry and lining them up on our kitchen counter. With the help of an ancient cookbook and a little red food coloring, we made the most delicious cake I had ever tasted. It was an incredible revelation that sacks of flour and sugar sitting dormant in back of our kitchen cabinets could create such unforgettable sweetness. Just by mixing those hidden and taken-for-granted treasures together, we built the foundation of a masterpiece that would put any packaged dessert to shame.

No matter how much time passes, I still get excited baking the cookies, muffins, and desserts I grew up making with Minnie. Anticipating the wonderful aromas that will envelope my kitchen and envisioning the delight a fresh batch of cookies inspires, I feel the warmth of Minnie's eternal presence beside me. These delicious re-creations have a special place in my heart because I know each recipe includes a secret ingredient: love. Perhaps this explains why fresh-baked treats are the ultimate comfort foods. The recipes that mean the most to us are the ones we grew up with, the ones that bring us home, the ones that remind us we are loved.

Surprisingly, these familiar recipes are often the hardest to find. Now the search is over. You'll find all of your favorite recipes here, from cookies and cakes for everyday desserts, to pumpkin pie and cranberry bread to create the perfect Thanksgiving, to gingerbread and Christmas cookies for a taste of the holidays. The easy-to-follow instructions, tips, and techniques guarantee success. Beginning with hints on how to choose equipment and ingredients and ending with the recipe for the fastest cleanup on record, you'll find that baking is simpler than you ever thought possible.

Whether you become an everyday baker or just bake on holidays and special occasions, these are the recipes you'll use over and over. Now let's bake!

BASICS

For the first time, recipes for the most loved muffins, cookies, cakes, pies, and breads are contained in one book. While the recipe names should all be familiar, some techniques might be new to beginning bakers. Beating egg whites, frosting cakes, making pie crusts, and kneading bread are quite easily accomplished by bakers of all levels and should neither be avoided nor feared. To make this book more helpful to those of you who are a little unsure around the kitchen, each chapter begins with information on what equipment to use and how to choose ingredients. If I recommend a particular ingredient or method, I always try to explain why. If a new technique is introduced in some of the recipes, I have provided detailed, foolproof directions in the chapter's introduction.

Before moving on to the individual chapters, it is essential to first familiarize yourself with the "basics." This chapter gives you an overview of the baking process. It has been said that baking is part art, part science. Although the way ingredients are combined and the proportion of one ingredient to another determine the taste and texture of the finished product, there is often room for adaptation and variation. The more you understand the relationship between ingredients and the reasons for accurate measuring and mixing, the more you can explore the art of baking and presenting your creations.

The most important thing to remember is that baking should be fun. Whether you're whipping up a batch muffins for a weekend breakfast, making cookies for an afternoon snack, or celebrating the fall's harvest with a freshly baked apple pie, relax and enjoy yourself. There are few things as treasured as a homemade treat.

Equipment

- Buy the best quality equipment you can afford; sturdier equipment will last longer.
- The essentials for most recipes include measuring cups and spoons, mixing bowls, baking pans or sheets, and cooling racks. Additional equipment includes a spatula, sturdy mixing spoon, sharp knife, whisk, grater, electric mixer, food processor, rolling pin, and timer.
- Nonstick cookware makes cleanup easier. Protect the non-stick coating by using plastic or wooden utensils.
- A microwave is a great baking aid. It softens butter to room temperature in about fifteen to twenty seconds and melts a stick of butter in about a minute.
- Invest in an oven thermometer to make sure your oven is heating properly. A hanging mercury thermometer is the most reliable. Oven temperatures that are too low will prevent cakes from fully rising, keep cookies from browning, and stop pie crusts from becoming crisp. Oven temperatures that are too high cause cakes to brown on the surface before the center is cooked, and result in overcooked or burned muffins and cookies. Check the temperature in different areas of your oven to make sure it has consistent heat. If you notice heat discrepancies, adjust cooking time or temperature to compensate. Most utility companies will recalibrate your oven at no cost.

The First Book of Baking

Ingredients

- Try not to substitute ingredients listed in the recipe.
- Always use high-quality ingredients. An ingredient that doesn't taste good by itself won't taste good when baked.
- Make sure fruit is ripe and flavorful, dairy products are fresh, and flavorings are the best available.
- Use pure extracts, not imitation, for more authentic flavor.
- Use fresh and fragrant spices. Store spices tightly covered in a cool and dry place for better and longer-lasting flavor.
- Use only the best-tasting real chocolate. Look for white chocolate made with cocoa butter, not tropical oils.
- Use fresh nuts. Old nuts can turn rancid. It is best to store nuts in an airtight container, preferably in the freezer or refrigerator. Bring nuts to room temperature before using. Toasting nuts until golden enhances their flavor and makes them more crisp.
- Nonstick vegetable sprays are a quick and convenient way to grease baking pans.

FLOUR

- Bleached and unbleached all-purpose flour can be used interchangeably. However, bleached all-purpose flour produces slightly lighter, puffier, and softer products than unbleached flour because it contains less protein. Protein absorbs liquid during mixing and forms gluten, a network of elastic strands that expands until firmed by the oven's heat. While strong gluten development is good for bread, which should have a chewy texture, it is not good for muffins, cookies, pie crusts, and cakes. This is why some delicate cakes call for cake flour, the flour with the least amount of protein, while bread flour's higher protein count is recommended for bread making.

- It is not necessary to sift flour unless noted.
- Do not use self-rising flour in any of the recipes in this book.

FATS

- The fat in a recipe adds flavor, binds, tenderizes, and controls the shape of baked goods. You can use either unsalted butter, salted butter, or margarine in most recipes, although unsalted butter produces a more authentic bakery taste. Do not use tub or "light" butter or margarine substitutes. When oil is called for, use unflavored oil—such as canola, corn, or safflower—unless otherwise specified.

SWEETENERS

- Sugar adds sweetness and tenderizes baked goods. It also adds color (browning is caused by sugar caramelizing).
- Brown sugar is granulated sugar that contains molasses. Although dark brown sugar contains slightly more molasses, light and dark brown sugar can be used interchangeably unless noted.
- Confectioners' sugar, also known as powdered sugar, is powdered granulated sugar mixed with a small amount of cornstarch to prevent clumping. Confectioners' sugar is often used in frostings.

EGGS

- Eggs add richness, moisture, flavor, color, and structure to batters.
- Beaten eggs aerate the batter, help it rise, and give it texture.
- The recipes in this book call for USDA large eggs.

LEAVENING

- Baking powder and baking soda can be used individually or in combination.

The First Book of Baking

- When baking powder or baking soda is mixed with other ingredients, a chemical reaction produces carbon dioxide, which lightens and aerates the batter.
- Baking soda reacts with acid ingredients like buttermilk and brown sugar.
- Double-acting baking powder reacts twice during the baking process, once when added to liquids and again when exposed to heat. If using baking powder, bake soon after mixing to take full advantage of its leavening power.
- When buying baking powder or soda, write the date of purchase on the lid for future reference—there is a substantial loss of strength after one year, especially with baking powder.
- To test the strength of baking powder: Stir two teaspoons of baking powder into hot water. It should foam madly.
- To test the strength of baking soda: Mix one-and-one-half teaspoons with one tablespoon of vinegar. It should fizz.
- Yeast, living organisms activated by moisture and warmth, produces a much slower rise than baking powder or soda.
- Always check the expiration date when using packages of granulated yeast.
- To test the strength of yeast: Mix one package of dry yeast, one teaspoon of sugar, and one-quarter cup of lukewarm water (105 to 110 degrees F), and leave it in a warm, dry spot for five minutes. If the mixture bubbles and froths, the yeast is viable and can be used in the recipe.

Before Baking

- The first step to successful baking is to read through the entire recipe.
- Clear off your work space so that you have room to work.
- Prepare the oven. Position oven racks as directed in the recipe.

- If the recipe does not say how to place the racks, use the following rule of thumb: For muffins, cookies, cakes, and breads, set the rack in the middle if you're using one pan or baking sheet. If you're using additional pans or baking sheets, position the oven racks near the center of the oven, making sure to leave enough room between shelves for the heat to circulate. When baking pies, place the racks in the lower settings.
- Always preheat the oven for at least fifteen minutes before baking.
- Prepare the baking pan. Use a nonstick vegetable spray, or apply a small amount of softened butter or shortening to grease the pan. Lining a pan with parchment paper (available on rolls or in sheets) will prevent sticking and over-browning.
- Allow time for refrigerated ingredients, primarily eggs and butter, to come to room temperature (about 70 degrees F) before mixing, unless noted. This guarantees better blending, less chance of curdling, and superior texture in the finished product. Butter can be quickly softened by cutting it into small pieces or by using a microwave. Place eggs in very warm water for a few minutes to help them lose their chill.
- One of the oldest principles of French cooking, and a rule among professional kitchens, is *mise en place,* which means "everything in place." This time-saving procedure means that you have all the equipment ready and all the ingredients prepared and measured before beginning a recipe. In home kitchens this means completing additional preparation, if needed (chopping, peeling, toasting, and so forth), and measuring the ingredients before you begin assembling the recipe. This eliminates any surprises during the baking process (such as suddenly discovering that you're out of vanilla or that you can't find your baking pan) and keeps the mixing process flowing without unnecessary interruptions.

The First Book of Baking

- Line up the ingredients, in the order in which they are listed in the recipe, before you begin. Move the ingredient aside after you have added it to the batter. This ensures nothing has been forgotten or added twice.

Measuring Ingredients

- Accurately measure all ingredients.
- Lightly spoon dry ingredients into a measuring cup and sweep off the excess with a knife. The exception is brown sugar, which should be firmly packed.
- It is most accurate to use smaller measuring cups instead of trying to gauge the measurement on a larger measuring cup. (For example, instead of trying to approximate three-quarters of a cup of flour using the inside mark on a one-cup measuring cup, use a one-half-cup measure and a one-quarter-cup measure.)
- Liquids are easiest to measure in a glass measuring cup read at eye level. Place the cup on a flat surface when adding ingredients.
- To prevent accidental overflows and eggshells in the batter, never measure ingredients over mixing bowls.

Baking

- Oven temperature usually varies about ten degrees within an oven, with the upper third and rear of the oven being the warmest. To ensure even baking, always reverse the pans from front to back; if you're baking on two racks, switch the pans from top to bottom during baking.
- Don't try to save time by increasing the oven temperature for faster results. You'll end up with an overcooked outside and undercooked inside.

- Always check during the second half of baking to make sure the baking process isn't further along than it should be, but try not to look in the oven more than is necessary. Opening and shutting the oven doors while baking affects the oven temperature, letting cooler air in and hot air out, and could cause cakes to fall or result in longer baking times.
- Trust your senses to let you know when baking is near completion. Wonderful aromas will fill the air. The batter will be solidifying and the top or edges will be lightly browned. The surface will feel firm and bounce back when lightly touched.
- Valuable moistness is lost by overbaking. Residual heat continues to bake the item after it is removed from the oven.
- After baking, it is best to place pans from the oven directly onto a cooling rack to allow air to circulate from all sides.

Keeping Clean

- Make your kitchen baking-friendly. Create a baking section in your cupboard to keep all your baking supplies and equipment together so they are easily accessible. Storing baking items together also shortens prep time and makes you more likely to think about baking!
- The more organized your kitchen is while you are preparing the recipe the easier it will be to clean.
- Keep a trash receptacle close by, and deposit all used wrappers and eggshells in it immediately. If a trash can isn't handy, place an empty box or mixing bowl on the counter near your work space.
- To eliminate messy spills and overflows, always use larger mixing bowls than you think will be necessary. This also prevents the need to transfer ingredients to a larger bowl midway into the recipe, creating additional cleanup.
- Use parchment paper to line your baking pans. Parchment paper prevents batters from sticking, so it helps keep pans

clean. When you're done baking, wipe off the parchment paper and store it for use the next time you bake.

- When grating zest, lightly oil the grater to prevent sticking. Grate directly over waxed paper for easier cleanup. Use a clean toothbrush to dislodge zest from the grater.
- When using honey or molasses, first coat your measuring utensil with a light application of oil or nonstick vegetable spray. The sticky liquid will pour out easily and make cleanup simple.
- Use a toothbrush or cotton swabs to clean hard-to-reach places.

After Baking

- Return each item to its proper place so it will be easy to find the next time you bake.
- Personalize your cookbooks to use as a guide for your future baking. On the recipe, note if the cooking instructions were accurate for your oven and if the amount of flavoring was right for you. To experiment with adding spices or flavorings, begin by adding a small amount, one-quarter to one-half teaspoon, and test until it satisfies your taste buds.
- Remember, small variations in measuring, oven temperature, or even the humidity or temperature in the kitchen can alter results, so don't be surprised if a recipe turns out slightly different on any given day.
- Enjoy the fruits of your labor!

Freezing

- To maintain maximum flavor and quality when freezing baked goods, make sure to wrap them airtight using foil, plastic wrap, zip-top bags, or plastic containers. Make sure the wrap and bags are designed for freezer use.

- Label and date everything before freezing so you can use it in a timely fashion.
- Keep a current list of freezer contents to refresh your memory.

Presentation

- Be dramatic and imaginative when presenting your desserts. Everything from a basic brownie to an unpretentious piece of pie will look majestic when placed on top of a beautifully decorated plate.
- Use garnishes and decorations with flavors that compliment the dessert or highlight one of its ingredients.
- Don't overdo the ornamentation. Use only one or two decorative elements at a time.
- Choose serving platters that will highlight the dessert. Look for interesting designs, colors, textures, shapes, and borders when choosing serving and dessert plates.
- Collect serving plates of different sizes and heights to use in combination when offering several desserts.
- Use oversized dessert plates to show off your creations.
- Practice the following design techniques to improve your skills.

Plate Decoration

- Instead of placing a dessert on an unadorned plate, drizzle or pipe melted chocolate or fruit purée on the serving plate or individual dessert plate. Write messages, make designs, or just use a random splashing of color and combination of tastes.
- To pipe without a pastry bag, fill a zip-top bag with melted chocolate or fruit purée, cut the tip off a corner, and squeeze designs onto plates. A condiment squeeze bottle with a narrow tip also works well.

- For easy fruit purées, process raspberries, kiwis, or mangos with sugar to taste (one to three tablespoons, depending on the sweetness of the fruit), and strain.
- Fruit purées or sauces can also be spooned onto the bottom of the plate so the dessert sits in the sauce. Use two sauces in combination for color or flavor contrasts (for example, kiwi and raspberry).
- If you're using two sauces, place them side by side, use one to outline the other, or make a pattern of dots, circles, or lines and drag a knife through them to create hearts, wisps, spiderwebs, and sunbursts.
- Dusting plates with cocoa (for light-colored plates) or confectioners' sugar (for dark plates) before placing the dessert on the plate makes it stand out. Spices like cinnamon and nutmeg can also be sprinkled for decoration.
- Use stencils to make precise designs out of cocoa, confectioners' sugar, or spices.
- Add fanned strawberries, cut up fresh fruit, chopped nuts, coffee beans, candied fruit peel, or toasted coconut to decorate a plate. Or place a dollop of whipped cream or crème fraîche on plates to make them more attractive. Chocolate-dipped fruit or nuts make an extra-special surprise.
- Use doilies, mint sprigs, or edible fresh flowers to decorate the serving plate.
- If inadvertent smudges occur during decorating, quickly wipe them off with a damp cloth before serving.

Dessert Decoration

- Enhance the finished dessert with simple or elaborate embellishments.
- For the most simple finishing touch, top pieces of cake or pie with a dollop or rosette of whipped cream, a sprinkling of confectioners' sugar, freshly cut fruit, or edible flowers.

- When using cocoa or confectioners' sugar as decoration, put one or two tablespoons in a wire strainer and shake lightly over cookies or cakes.
- A ribbon wrapped around a whole cake looks very professional.
- Use edible gold dust or foil for dramatic cake decorations (especially with chocolate cakes).

Chocolate Decorations

- *Grated chocolate:* Place a hand grater on foil or waxed paper. Rub a large piece of bittersweet or semisweet chocolate through the coarse side. Place chocolate shavings on dessert or dessert plate.
- *Chocolate curls:* Slightly soften a one-inch-thick bar of bittersweet, semisweet, or white chocolate. The chocolate should be soft and malleable, so that the curls will not crack when they are made, but it should not be melting. Hold the bar over a plate, shave the smooth side of the chocolate with a swivel vegetable peeler, and let the curled shavings drop onto the plate. Move the bar after making each curl so the curls are evenly spaced on the plate and do not touch. Place curls in the refrigerator or freezer until firm and you are ready to use them. If the chocolate begins to flake or break, soften it again.
- *Melted chocolate:* Drizzle the dessert with melted chocolate. To melt chocolate in the microwave, place uncovered chocolate in a glass measuring cup or microwave-safe bowl. Heat on high for one to two minutes, stirring every fifteen seconds to check its progress. When ready, the chocolate may not look melted but its appearance should change from dull to shiny. Stir until completely melted and smooth. If a few lumps remain, return it to the microwave for a few seconds. White chocolate can also be melted in the microwave on medium.

The First Book of Baking

Be sure to stir frequently. When melting chocolate over a burner, place chopped chocolate pieces in the top of a double boiler over hot, not boiling, water, stirring often. Do not allow any water or steam to come in contact with the chocolate or it will "seize" and become clumpy and gritty.

- *Chocolate leaves:* Use nonpoisonous leaves (unsprayed rose, lemon, geranium, and ivy work well) that have been washed and dried. To make the coating, melt four ounces of bittersweet, semisweet, or white chocolate. With a pastry brush or small spatula, spread a layer of melted chocolate about one-eighth inch thick onto the underside of the leaf, making sure none gets on the front of the leaf. Place the leaves on a baking sheet lined with foil or waxed paper, and refrigerate until set, about five minutes. Spread another thin layer of melted chocolate over the first layer. Refrigerate until the chocolate is firm. Carefully peel off the leaves, beginning at the stem ends, and discard. Refrigerate the chocolate leaves until ready to use.

- *Chocolate shapes:* Spread melted chocolate one-eighth inch thick on a flat cutting surface lined with parchment paper. Let it harden five to ten minutes. Using decorative cutters or a knife, cut the chocolate into shapes to use as decorations.

- *Chocolate scrolls:* Spread melted chocolate one-eighth inch thick on a flat cutting surface or an inverted baking sheet. Let it cool until firm, but not completely hard, about five to ten minutes. Push a pastry scraper or a wide, sharp-edged spatula across the chocolate, directed away from you. The blade will lift up the chocolate in scrolls the same width as the spatula. Use a toothpick to transfer the scrolls to the dessert. For marbled chocolate scrolls, melt two ounces of dark chocolate and two ounces of white chocolate. With a spatula, spread melted chocolate and white chocolate in several thin side-by-side strips.

Draw the blade through the chocolates to create a marbleized effect. Proceed as above.

- *Chocolate-coated nuts or fruits:* Melt chocolate and dip nuts or fruits entirely or partially into the chocolate. Cool on waxed paper until the chocolate has hardened.

Muffins and Quick Breads

❧ ❧

Muffins and quick breads, now more popular than ever, are the perfect way to start your morning. Most muffins take less than ten minutes to prepare and bake in less than half an hour. Quick breads, unlike yeast breads, which take several hours to rise, can be made and baked in about an hour.

Muffins, quick breads, scones, and biscuits are so adaptable. Try combining different fruits and flavorings to create your own favorite breakfast treat.

Equipment

Pans

- Use shiny pans that reflect heat for better color and more tender crusts.
- Muffin tins come in several sizes. The standard-size muffin tin has twelve cups, each of which holds about one-half cup of batter. Jumbo muffin tins have six cups, each of which holds one cup of batter. Most mini-muffin tins have twelve cups, each of which holds about one-eighth cup of batter.

- For quick breads, use a 9 by 5 by 3-inch loaf pan.
- Many muffin tins and loaf pans have nonstick finishes, which make cleanup easier.

OTHER EQUIPMENT

- A wire whisk and a sturdy mixing spoon are usually all you need to mix muffin ingredients.
- An electric mixer is helpful for a recipe that calls for softened butter and sugar to be creamed together.
- A food processor is handy for chopping and grating ingredients and for quickly making biscuits and scones.
- Cooling racks allow air to freely circulate on all sides of the muffins and breads to prevent overbaking.

Ingredients

- Use either bleached or unbleached all-purpose flour.
- Use unsalted butter for a more authentic bakery flavor. If a recipe calls for oil, use unflavored oils such as safflower or canola oil.
- Use USDA large eggs at room temperature. To quickly bring eggs to room temperature, place them in very warm water for five to ten minutes.
- Fresh fruit should be ripe and flavorful.
- Muffins and quick breads are very accommodating to adaptation. Use your imagination and experiment with combining flavors and ingredients to suit your own tastes. Start with small additions and build until you get the flavor combination you're searching for.

Making Muffins

- Prepare the oven. Position the oven rack in the middle of the oven.
- Always preheat the oven for at least fifteen minutes before baking.
- Prepare the baking pan. To prevent sticking, lightly grease muffin tins and top surface with vegetable spray, butter, or vegetable oil, or line tins with baking cups.
- Grease only the bottom of the loaf pans for a better formed loaf. As the batter rises during baking, it will "grow" by clinging to the sides of the pan.

MIXING THE BATTER

- Thoroughly mix dry ingredients and liquid ingredients separately with a whisk or spoon before combining them.
- Overmixing creates tough muffins, so blend just until dry ingredients are moistened (don't be afraid of lumps).
- For quick, freshly baked muffins in the morning, mix and store the dry and liquid ingredients separately the night before so they're ready to combine and bake when you wake. Refrigerate the liquid ingredients; if the recipe calls for melted butter, prepare it just before mixing.

FILLING THE PANS

- Fill muffin cups two-thirds full.
- For fewer spills, use a half-cup measuring cup or a number 8 ice cream scoop to fill muffin tins.

- Each muffin recipe in this chapter makes twelve standard muffins, six jumbo muffins, or thirty-six mini muffins. If you don't have enough batter to fill all the tins, place some water in the empties to prevent the pan from scorching.
- When filling loaf pans for quick breads, equally distribute the batter in the pan and smooth the top for even cooking.

BAKING

- To ensure even heating, rotate the pan from front to back midway during baking.
- Always check muffins and quick breads at least five minutes before the lower estimated cooking time to make sure they are not overcooking.
- To test for doneness, insert a toothpick or wooden skewer into the center of the muffin or bread. It should come out clean.
- If muffins or quick breads are browning on top too much, cover them with aluminum foil. If this occurs early during baking, decrease the oven temperature by twenty-five degrees.
- Experiment with different-sized muffin tins for variety. Giant muffins are great for weekend breakfasts. Miniature muffins are fun for parties and for snacks. Add five minutes to the baking time for giant muffins, reduce the baking time by ten minutes for miniatures.

COOLING AND SLICING

- To prevent soggy muffins, remove them from the tins and place them on the cooling rack as soon as they are cool enough to handle.
- To keep muffins warm, angle them in their cups to allow steam to escape.

- Cool quick breads completely on a rack for easier slicing.
- Many quick breads (especially fruit and nut breads) improve in flavor if baked a day ahead of serving.

STORING

- Store muffins or quick breads tightly wrapped at room temperature. Cool completely before wrapping.
- Muffins and quick breads can be stored in the freezer for several months if well wrapped. Cool completely before wrapping.

REHEATING

- To reheat frozen muffins in the oven, wrap them in foil and heat at 350 degrees F for about ten minutes.
- To reheat frozen muffins in the microwave, heat them uncovered on high for forty to fifty seconds, then let them stand for thirty seconds.
- Frozen quick breads are best thawed at room temperature.

Date-Nut Bread

༂ ᡐ

¼	cup (½ stick) butter, cut into chunks
1	cup dates, pitted and coarsely chopped
⅔	cup brown sugar, firmly packed
¾	cup boiling water
2	cups all-purpose flour
2	teaspoons baking powder
1	teaspoon baking soda
½	teaspoon salt
2	eggs, beaten
1	cup walnuts, coarsely chopped

This fruity nut-filled bread tastes wonderful with cream cheese and a hot cup of tea on a winter's day.

Prep Time: 15 to 20 minutes
Baking Time: 40 to 50 minutes
Equipment: 9 by 5 by 3-inch loaf pan, measuring spoons, measuring cups, large bowl, medium bowl, spatula, cooling rack

1. Preheat the oven to 350 degrees F. Lightly grease the bottom only of a 9 by 5 by 3-inch loaf pan.
2. In a large bowl, combine the butter, dates, and brown sugar. Pour in the boiling water and stir. Let the mixture sit for 10 minutes.
3. Meanwhile, in a medium bowl, mix the flour, baking powder, baking soda, and salt.
4. When the date mixture has cooled, add the eggs and mix well.
5. Add the dry ingredients to the date mixture and stir until just combined.
6. Add the walnuts. Do not overmix.
7. Scrape the batter into the prepared pan. Smooth the top with a spatula.
8. Bake 40 to 50 minutes, or until a toothpick inserted in the center comes out clean.
9. Cool 5 minutes. Loosen the sides of the loaf from the pan and remove. Cool completely on a rack before slicing.

Yield: 1 loaf, approximately 12 to 14 slices

VARIATION

Extra-Fruity Date-Nut Bread: *Add ¹/₂ cup raisins or other dried fruit with the nuts (step 6).*

TIPS

The flavor of nut bread improves with time, so bake this a day ahead if possible.

Chopping dates can be a messy job. Lightly coat your knife or kitchen shears with oil, or frequently dip them in water, to prevent the dates from sticking to the metal. When chopping dates in a food processor, add a few tablespoons of the flour from the recipe to stop the dates from sticking.

You can store dates in a tightly sealed container in the refrigerator for several months or in the freezer for up to a year.

Packaged dates are sometimes coated with a little sugar or flour to prevent the fruit from sticking together in the package, but this small amount won't affect recipes.

Lemon–Poppy Seed Muffins

Muffins

2	cups all-purpose flour
2/3	cup granulated sugar
1	tablespoon baking powder
1	teaspoon baking soda
1/2	teaspoon salt
2	tablespoons poppy seeds
2	eggs
1/2	cup (1 stick) butter, melted
1	cup milk
1	tablespoon lemon zest, grated
1/3	cup fresh lemon juice

Glaze

1/3	cup fresh lemon juice
3	tablespoons sugar

Poppy seeds give these aromatic lemon muffins an interesting texture.

Prep Time: 10 to 15 minutes
Baking Time: 20 to 25 minutes
Equipment: muffin tin, measuring spoons, measuring cups, grater, large bowl, medium bowl, small bowl, cooling rack (pastry brush, optional)

1. Preheat the oven to 400 degrees F. Lightly grease a muffin tin, including the top edges.
2. In a large bowl, mix the flour, sugar, baking powder, baking soda, salt, and poppy seeds. Make a well in the center. Set aside.
3. In a medium bowl, beat the eggs. Add the butter, milk, lemon zest, and lemon juice, and mix until blended. Pour the mixture into the well of dry ingredients and stir until just combined. Do not overmix.
4. Spoon the batter into the prepared muffin cups, dividing evenly.
5. Bake 20 to 25 minutes, or until the tops are golden and a toothpick inserted in the center comes out clean.
6. Meanwhile, prepare the glaze. In a small bowl, stir the lemon juice and sugar until the sugar dissolves. Set aside.

7. When the muffins are done, remove them from the oven and pierce the tops repeatedly with a toothpick. Stir the glaze again and slowly drizzle it (or brush with a pastry brush) over each muffin.

8. Allow the muffins to absorb the glaze for about 10 minutes. Remove them from the tin, cool slightly on a rack, and serve.

Yield: 12 muffins

VARIATION

Fruity Lemon Muffins: *Replace the poppy seeds with 1 1/2 cups whole blueberries or raspberries.*

TIPS

One medium lemon yields almost one-quarter cup of juice and about one tablespoon of grated zest.

To get more juice from a lemon, microwave it on high for ten seconds or put it in a bowl of hot water for thirty minutes. Then roll it on the counter, pressing lightly, before squeezing the juice. This breaks up the membrane inside the lemon so that the juices will release more easily when squeezed.

Always grate the lemon zest before squeezing the lemon for juice.

Grate only the yellow portion of the lemon peel. The white portion, known as the pith, is very bitter.

Soaking poppy seeds in milk for an hour or more brings out their flavor. Add the poppy seed and milk combination when the milk is called for.

Banana–Nut Muffins

1 1/2 cups all-purpose flour
3/4 cup granulated sugar
2 teaspoons baking powder
1 teaspoon baking soda
1/2 teaspoon salt
1 egg
1/2 cup (1 stick) butter, melted
1 cup milk
1 1/2 cups bananas, mashed (about 3 medium)
3/4 cup walnuts, coarsely chopped

When you don't feel like monkeying around in the morning, there's nothing better to make than these muffins. They're quick to prepare and are a delicious way to use up overripe bananas.

Prep Time: 10 to 15 minutes
Baking Time: 20 to 25 minutes
Equipment: muffin tin, measuring spoons, measuring cups, large bowl, medium bowl, cooling rack

1. Preheat the oven to 400 degrees F. Lightly grease a muffin tin, including the top edges.
2. In a large bowl, mix the flour, sugar, baking powder, baking soda, and salt. Make a well in the center. Set aside.
3. In a medium bowl, beat the egg. Add the butter, milk, and bananas, and mix until blended. Pour the mixture into the well of dry ingredients and stir until just combined.
4. Add the walnuts. Do not overmix.
5. Spoon the batter into the prepared muffin cups, dividing evenly.
6. Bake 20 to 25 minutes, or until the tops are golden and a toothpick inserted in the center comes out clean.
7. Cool muffins in their tin for 5 minutes. Remove the muffins from the tin, cool slightly on a rack, and serve.

Yield: 12 muffins

Spiced Banana-Nut Muffins: *Add $^1/_4$ teaspoon ginger, $^1/_4$ teaspoon cinnamon, and $^1/_4$ teaspoon nutmeg to the dry ingredients (step 2).*

TIPS

Use only ripe or overripe bananas for rich banana flavor.

A potato masher works great for mashing bananas. Be sure to leave some chunks.

Plan ahead. When you have extra bananas that you can't use right away, mash them with a little lemon juice and store in an airtight container in the freezer until you're ready to make the muffins.

Pumpkin Bread

ॐ ॐ

2	cups all-purpose flour
1	cup granulated sugar
2	teaspoons baking powder
$\frac{1}{2}$	teaspoon baking soda
$\frac{1}{2}$	teaspoon salt
1	teaspoon ground cinnamon
$\frac{1}{2}$	teaspoon ground nutmeg
$\frac{1}{2}$	teaspoon ground cloves
$\frac{1}{2}$	cup raisins
2	eggs
$\frac{1}{2}$	cup (1 stick) butter, melted
$\frac{1}{3}$	cup water
1	cup (8 ounces) pumpkin, canned unsweetened or puréed fresh cooked

This moist and aromatic pumpkin bread is a Thanksgiving classic.

Prep Time: 10 to 15 minutes
Baking Time: 50 to 60 minutes
Equipment: 9 by 5 by 3-inch loaf pan, measuring spoons, measuring cups, large bowl, medium bowl, spatula, cooling rack

1. Preheat the oven to 350 degrees F. Lightly grease the bottom only of a 9 by 5 by 3-inch loaf pan.
2. In a large bowl, mix the flour, sugar, baking powder, baking soda, salt, cinnamon, nutmeg, cloves, and raisins. Make a well in the center. Set aside.
3. In a medium bowl, beat the eggs. Add the butter, water, and pumpkin, and mix until blended. Pour the mixture into the well of dry ingredients and stir until just combined. Do not overmix. The batter will be thick.
4. Scrape the batter into the prepared pan. Smooth the top with a spatula.
5. Bake 50 to 60 minutes, or until a toothpick inserted in the center comes out clean.
6. Cool 5 minutes. Loosen the sides of the loaf from the pan and remove. Cool completely on a rack before slicing.

Yield: 1 loaf, approximately 12 to 14 slices

Goldenly Fruity: *Use golden raisins for a special presentation.*

TIPS

To prepare fresh pumpkin, cut one pound of peeled pumpkin meat into half-inch pieces. Steam the pumpkin for twenty-five minutes, or micro-wave for ten minutes, stirring occasionally for even cooking. Cool to room temperature and purée.

Blueberry Muffins

2 cups all-purpose flour
3/4 cup granulated sugar
1 tablespoon baking powder
1/2 teaspoon salt
2 cups blueberries
2 eggs
1/2 cup (1 stick) butter, melted
1 cup milk

During blueberry season there are few better uses for fresh berries than these muffins. Brimming with fruit, it's no wonder they're such a favorite.

Prep Time: 10 to 15 minutes
Baking Time: 20 to 25 minutes
Equipment: muffin tin, measuring spoons, measuring cups, large bowl, medium bowl, cooling rack

1. Preheat the oven to 400 degrees F. Lightly grease a muffin tin, including the top edges.
2. In a large bowl, mix the flour, sugar, baking powder, salt, and blueberries. Make a well in the center. Set aside.
3. In a medium bowl, beat the eggs. Add the butter and milk, and mix until blended. Pour the mixture into the well of dry ingredients and stir until just combined. Do not overmix.
4. Spoon the batter into the prepared muffin cups, dividing evenly.
5. Bake 20 to 25 minutes, or until the tops are golden and a toothpick inserted in the center comes out clean.
6. Cool the muffins in their tin for 5 minutes. Remove the muffins from the tin, cool slightly on a rack, and serve.

Yield: 12 muffins

Streusel-Topped Muffins: *Mix 1/2 cup melted butter, 1/2 cup sugar, 1/2 teaspoon cinnamon, and 1 cup flour. Crumble the mixture and sprinkle it on the muffins before baking.*

Citrus Zest: *For a mild citrus flavor, add either the grated zest of an orange or a lemon to the batter (step 3).*

Sugar and Spice: *Combine 3 tablespoons sugar and 1 teaspoon cinnamon. Sprinkle the mixture on top of the muffins before baking.*

TIPS

You can use either fresh or frozen blueberries.

Coating the blueberries with flour prevents them from falling to the bottom of the muffin.

Keep a bag of blueberries in your freezer so you can enjoy these muffins year-round.

Spread washed fresh berries on a baking sheet and freeze. When frozen, store them in air-tight bags.

To prevent blueberry juice from turning your muffins gray, do not thaw frozen berries before adding to batter.

Make sure frozen blueberries are loose, like little marbles, instead of a large mass.

Do not be tempted to overload the muffins with blueberries. Too many berries make muffins soggy and formless.

Bran Muffins

1½ cups wheat bran
1½ cups all-purpose flour
¼ cup brown sugar, firmly
    packed
1 tablespoon baking
    powder
½ teaspoon baking soda
½ teaspoon salt
1 cup raisins
2 eggs
1 cup buttermilk
¼ cup (½ stick) butter,
    melted
¼ cup honey
¼ cup molasses

These hearty muffins are full of raisins and are sweetened with brown sugar, honey, and molasses.

Prep Time: 10 to 15 minutes
Baking Time: 20 to 25 minutes
Equipment: muffin tin, measuring spoons, measuring cups, large bowl, medium bowl, cooling rack

1. Preheat the oven to 400 degrees F. Lightly grease a muffin tin, including the top edges.
2. In a large bowl, mix the bran, flour, brown sugar, baking powder, baking soda, salt, and raisins. Make a well in the center. Set aside.
3. In a medium bowl, beat the eggs. Add the buttermilk, butter, honey, and molasses, and mix until blended. Pour the mixture into the well of dry ingredients and stir until just combined. Do not overmix.
4. Spoon the batter into the prepared muffin cups, dividing evenly.
5. Bake 20 to 25 minutes, or until the tops are firm and a toothpick inserted in the center comes out clean.
6. Cool muffins in their tins for 5 minutes. Remove the muffins from the tin, cool slightly on a rack, and serve.

Yield: 12 muffins

Citrus Zest: *For a mild citrus flavor, add the grated zest of an orange to the batter (step 3).*

TIPS

Coating the raisins with flour prevents them from falling to the bottom of the muffins.

For a more interesting presentation, use both dark and golden raisins.

Wheat bran is sold in most supermarkets and health food stores.

Muffins and Quick Breads

Scones

ҽ҂ ҂ҽ

2 cups all-purpose flour
¼ cup granulated sugar
1 tablespoon baking
  powder
½ teaspoon salt
½ cup (1 stick) butter,
  chilled and cut into
  large pieces
¾ cup milk
1 cup raisins
1 egg, well beaten

These scones are lighter than most, and so delicious. Made in the food processor, they are a snap to prepare.

Prep Time: 5 to 10 minutes
Baking Time: 13 to 18 minutes
Equipment: baking sheet, food processor, measuring spoons, measuring cups, cooling rack

1. Preheat the oven to 400 degrees F. Lightly grease a baking sheet.
2. In food processor fitted with metal chopping blade, add flour, sugar, baking powder, and salt. Pulse to combine (about four pulses).
3. Add the butter and pulse until the mixture resembles coarse crumbs (about ten pulses).
4. Add the milk and pulse until just combined and evenly moistened (about eight pulses). Do not allow the dough to form a ball.
5. Transfer the dough to a large bowl and stir in the raisins. Do not overmix. The dough will be sticky.
6. Divide the dough into 8 equal pieces and place them on the baking sheet, leaving 2 inches between scones.
7. Flatten slightly and brush lightly with egg.
8. Bake 13 to 18 minutes, or until golden and the tops are firm.
9. Remove the scones from the baking sheet, cool slightly on a rack, and serve.

Yield: 8 scones

VARIATIONS

Double Raisin Scones: *Use a combination of golden and dark raisins.*

Truly Fruity Scones: *Substitute blueberries, dried cranberries, or dried cherries for the raisins.*

TIPS

If a food processor is not available, use your fingertips or a pastry blender to combine butter and dry ingredients.

For more evenly shaped scones, roll out the dough $^3/_4$ inch thick and cut out scones with 4-inch-round cutters. For triangle-shaped scones, press the dough into a $^3/_4$-inch-thick circle and cut into equal-sized wedges.

For slightly sweeter scones, sprinkle sugar on top of the dough before baking.

Biscuits

꿍 ᢏᢙ

2 cups all-purpose flour
1 tablespoon baking
    powder
½ teaspoon salt
5 tablespoons butter,
    chilled and cut into
    large pieces
¾ cup milk, plus extra for
    glazing

Whether they're topped with scrambled eggs and bacon for breakfast or served with fried chicken and gravy for dinner, these light, flaky biscuits are a welcome addition to any meal. Biscuits are best served hot from the oven, so time them appropriately. Use a food processor for quick mixing.

Prep Time: 5 to 10 minutes
Baking Time: 13 to 18 minutes
Equipment: baking sheet, food processor, measuring spoons, measuring cups

1. Preheat the oven to 450 degrees F. Take out a baking sheet.
2. In a food processor fitted with a metal chopping blade, add the flour, baking powder, and salt. Pulse to combine (about four pulses).
3. Add the butter and pulse until the mixture resembles coarse crumbs (about eight pulses).
4. Add the milk and pulse until just combined and evenly moistened (about five pulses). Do not allow the dough to form a ball.
5. Transfer the dough to a lightly floured surface. Knead for about 30 seconds, pushing the dough with the palms of your hands, to make the dough less sticky.
6. Pat or gently roll the dough ½ inch thick. Cut out biscuits using a lightly floured 3-inch-round cutter or a knife. Press the scraps together and pat the dough ½ inch thick to make additional biscuits.

The First Book of Baking

7. Transfer the biscuits to an ungreased baking sheet and brush the tops with milk.
8. Bake 13 to 18 minutes, or until golden and the tops are firm.
9. Remove the biscuits from the baking sheet and serve immediately.

Yield: 8 to 10 biscuits

VARIATIONS

Buttermilk Biscuits: *Buttermilk, a form of lowfat milk, has a tangy flavor and gives breads a lighter, fluffier texture. For delicious buttermilk biscuits, add ¹/₂ teaspoon baking soda and 1 teaspoon sugar to the dry ingredients (step 2). Increase the butter to 6 tablespoons, and substitute buttermilk for milk.*

Flavored Biscuits: *Liven up biscuits by adding 1 teaspoon or more (depending on personal taste) of one of the following to the batter in step 4: black pepper, chopped fresh herbs, paprika, dry mustard, or grated cheese.*

TIPS

Biscuits can also be made easily by hand. Combine dry ingredients in a large bowl. Add the butter and work the mixture with your fingertips until it resembles coarse crumbs. Add the milk and stir gently until just combined. Continue with step 5.

Instead of rolling and cutting the biscuits, you can drop the dough from a large spoon onto the baking sheet.

For a biscuit that's easier to split, roll the dough ¹/₄ inch thick and fold it in half before you cut out the biscuits. After baking, it will easily separate at the fold.

For soft-sided biscuits, bake them close together.

For crusty biscuits, bake them on a sideless pan and place them one inch apart.

Biscuits don't have to be round. Be creative—you can cut them into any shape you like.

Cranberry–Orange Bread

Bread

2 cups all-purpose flour
¾ cup granulated sugar
2 teaspoons baking powder
½ teaspoon baking soda
½ teaspoon salt
2 eggs
¼ cup orange juice, freshly squeezed
¼ cup (½ stick) butter, melted
2 teaspoons orange zest, grated (about 1 large orange)
1 cup buttermilk
1½ cups whole cranberries

Glaze

¼ cup orange juice, freshly squeezed
3 tablespoons sugar

Not only is this bread perfect for Thanksgiving, it's so good you'll want to keep a bag of cranberries in the freezer so you can make it all year.

Prep Time: 10 to 15 minutes
Baking Time: 50 to 60 minutes
Equipment: 9 by 5 by 3-inch loaf pan, measuring spoons, measuring cups, grater, large bowl, medium bowl, spatula, small bowl, cooling rack (pastry brush, optional)

1. Preheat the oven to 350 degrees F. Lightly grease the bottom only of a 9 by 5 by 3-inch loaf pan.
2. In a large bowl, mix the flour, sugar, baking powder, baking soda, and salt. Make a well in the center. Set aside.
3. In a medium bowl, beat the eggs. Add the orange juice, butter, orange zest, and buttermilk, and mix until blended. Pour the mixture into the well of dry ingredients and stir until just combined.
4. Add the cranberries. Do not overmix.
5. Scrape the batter into the prepared pan. Smooth the top with a spatula.
6. Bake 50 to 60 minutes, or until a toothpick inserted in the center comes out clean.
7. Meanwhile, prepare the glaze. In a small bowl, stir the orange juice and sugar until the sugar dissolves. Set aside.

8. When the bread is done, remove it from the oven and pierce the top repeatedly with a toothpick or wooden skewer. Stir the glaze again and slowly drizzle it (or brush with a pastry brush) over the top of the bread.

9. Cool 5 minutes. Loosen the sides of the loaf from the pan and remove. Cool completely on a rack before slicing.

Yield: 1 loaf, approximately 12 to 14 slices

VARIATION

Incredibly Nutty Cranberry Bread: *Add ¹/₂ cup chopped nuts with the cranberries (step 4).*

TIPS

Use frozen cranberries directly from the freezer. Don't thaw.

Always grate the orange before squeezing it for juice.

Popovers

1   cup all-purpose flour
1   cup milk
2   eggs
½   teaspoon salt
1   tablespoon butter,
       melted

Popovers get their shape from the steam that forms inside of them while they bake. They get their name because they "pop over" the edge of the pan as they bake.

Prep Time: 5 to 10 minutes
Baking Time: 35 minutes
Equipment: muffin tin, measuring spoons, measuring cup, food processor or blender

1. Preheat the oven to 400 degrees F. Generously grease a muffin tin.
2. In a food processor or blender, combine the flour, milk, eggs, salt, and butter. Process until smooth (scraping down the sides, if necessary).
3. Fill the muffin cups two-thirds full with batter and place in the center of the oven.
4. Bake for 35 minutes, or until puffed, golden, and crisp. Do not open the oven door while the popovers are baking.
5. Serve immediately.

Yield: 8 to 10 popovers

Flavored Popovers: *Dress up popovers by adding $1/4$ cup chopped fresh chives or $1/3$ cup grated Parmesan cheese with $1/2$ teaspoon dried basil or dill to the batter (step 2).*

TIPS

If you don't have a food processor or blender, you can make popovers using a whisk or rotary beater. Make sure to mix the batter until smooth.

Custard cups or popover cups can be used instead of a muffin tin. Use six- or seven-ounce cups and fill them two-thirds full.

Remember, if the oven door does not remain closed for the duration of baking, the popovers might fall.

For extra-crispy popovers, let the popovers bake completely. Then make a slit in the top to let out steam and bake the popovers at 350 degrees F for an additional ten minutes.

Banana Bread

2 cups all-purpose flour
1 teaspoon baking powder
1 teaspoon baking soda
½ teaspoon salt
½ cup (1 stick) butter, softened
¾ cup granulated sugar
2 eggs
1 ½ cups bananas, mashed (about 3 wmedium)
½ cup walnuts, coarsely chopped

Everyone goes bananas over freshly baked banana bread. This easy to make bread is a great way to recycle leftover or overripe bananas.

Prep Time: 10 to 15 minutes
Baking Time: 50 to 60 minutes
Equipment: 9 by 5 by 3-inch loaf pan, measuring spoons, measuring cups, large bowl, medium bowl, spatula, cooling rack (electric mixer, optional)

1. Preheat the oven to 350 degrees F. Lightly grease the bottom only of a 9 by 5 by 3-inch loaf pan.
2. In a medium bowl, mix the flour, baking powder, baking soda, and salt. Set aside.
3. In a large bowl, using a sturdy spoon or an electric mixer, cream the butter and sugar until thoroughly combined and fluffy (about 1 minute).
4. Add the eggs and beat until smooth. Mix in the bananas.
5. Blend in the dry ingredients until just combined.
6. Add the walnuts. Do not overmix. The batter will be thick and lumpy.
7. Scrape the batter into the prepared pan. Smooth the top with a spatula.
8. Bake 50 to 60 minutes, or until a toothpick inserted in the center comes out clean.
9. Cool 5 minutes. Loosen the sides of the loaf from the pan and remove. Cool completely on a rack before slicing.

Yield: 1 loaf, approximately 12 to 14 slices

Incredibly Nutty Bread: *Sprinkle an additional $1/2$ cup chopped walnuts on top of the loaf before baking.*

Sugar and Spice: *Combine 3 tablespoons sugar and 1 teaspoon cinnamon. Sprinkle the mixture on top of the bread before baking.*

When in France: *Banana bread makes great French toast!*

TIPS

The easiest way to cream butter and sugar is with an electric mixer. Otherwise, use a sturdy spoon or your hands.

Use only ripe or overripe bananas for rich banana flavor.

A potato masher works great for mashing bananas. Be sure to leave some chunks.

Plan ahead. When you have extra bananas that you can't use right away, mash them with a little lemon juice and store in an airtight container in the freezer until you're ready to make banana bread.

Zucchini Bread

ཨཾ ཨཾ

2 cups all-purpose flour
1 cup granulated sugar
2 teaspoons baking powder
½ teaspoon baking soda
½ teaspoon salt
1 teaspoon ground cinnamon
½ teaspoon ground cloves (optional)
2 eggs
½ cup vegetable oil
¼ cup water
2 cups zucchini, unpeeled and grated (about 1 large zucchini)

This bread should be a staple in the summer when zucchini is plentiful. Zucchini adds moistness and texture to this deliciously fragrant bread.

Prep Time: 10 to 15 minutes
Baking Time: 50 to 60 minutes
Equipment: 9 by 5 by 3-inch loaf pan, measuring spoons, measuring cups, grater, large bowl, medium bowl, spatula, cooling rack

1. Preheat the oven to 350 degrees F. Lightly grease the bottom only of a 9 by 5 by 3-inch loaf pan.
2. In a large bowl, mix the flour, sugar, baking powder, baking soda, salt, cinnamon, and cloves. Make a well in the center. Set aside.
3. In a medium bowl, beat the eggs. Add the oil and water and mix until blended. Pour the mixture into the well of dry ingredients and stir until just combined.
4. Add the zucchini. Do not overmix. The batter will be thick.
5. Scrape the batter into the prepared pan. Smooth the top with a spatula.
6. Bake 50 to 60 minutes, or until a toothpick inserted in the center comes out clean.
7. Cool 5 minutes. Loosen the sides of the loaf from the pan and remove. Cool completely on a rack before slicing.

Yield: 1 loaf, approximately 12 to 14 slices

Variations

Incredibly Nutty Bread: *Add $^1/_2$ cup chopped nuts with the zucchini (step 4).*

Raisinably Better Bread: *Add $^1/_2$ cup of raisins to the dry ingredients (step 2).*

Tips

Use a food processor fitted with a shredding blade to shred zucchini quickly.

For extra-quick prep time, shred the zucchini before you start the recipe.

Muffins and Quick Breads

Corn Muffins

1 ¼ cups all-purpose flour
1 ¼ cups yellow cornmeal
2 tablespoons sugar
2 teaspoons baking
   powder
½ teaspoon baking soda
1 teaspoon salt
2 eggs
¼ cup (½ stick) butter,
   melted
1 cup milk

Corn muffins are very versatile—there are so many ways to zip them up. These muffins are not too sweet and have a great cornmeal flavor.

Prep Time: 10 to 15 minutes
Baking Time: 15 to 20 minutes
Equipment: muffin tin, measuring spoons, measuring cups, large bowl, medium bowl, cooling rack

1. Preheat the oven to 400 degrees F. Lightly grease a muffin tin, including the top edges.
2. In a large bowl, mix the flour, cornmeal, sugar, baking powder, baking soda, and salt. Make a well in the center. Set aside.
3. In a medium bowl, beat the eggs. Add the butter and milk, and mix until blended. Pour the mixture into the well of dry ingredients and stir until just combined. Do not overmix.
4. Spoon the batter into the prepared muffin cups, dividing evenly.
5. Bake 15 to 20 minutes, or until the tops are golden and a toothpick inserted in the center comes out clean.
6. Cool the muffins in their tin for 5 minutes. Remove the muffins from the tin, cool slightly on a rack, and serve.

Yield: 12 muffins

Savory Corn Muffins: *Use any one or a combination of these add-ins for extra flavor: 1 1/2 cups whole corn kernels; 1 cup shredded cheddar cheese or Monterey Jack cheese; 1 or 2 diced green chili peppers; 1/4 cup chopped fresh herbs (parsley, chives, tarragon); 1 tablespoon freshly ground black pepper; 1/2 cup chopped green onion; 1 cup diced crisp-cooked bacon.*

Sweet Corn Muffins: *For a sweeter muffin, increase the sugar to 1/4 cup, increase the flour to 1 1/2 cups, and decrease the cornmeal to 1 cup.*

Fruity Corn Muffins: *Add 1 1/2 cups whole blueberries or raspberries to the dry ingredients.*

Colored Corn Muffins: *Use white or blue cornmeal instead of yellow.*

Chocolate Chip Muffins

~ ~

2 cups all-purpose flour
½ cup granulated sugar
1 tablespoon baking
  powder
½ teaspoon salt
1 egg
1 cup milk
⅓ cup vegetable oil
1 cup semisweet
  chocolate chips

These chip-filled muffins are a guilt-free way to enjoy chocolate for breakfast!

Prep Time: 5 to 10 minutes
Baking Time: 20 to 25 minutes
Equipment: muffin tin, measuring spoons, measuring cups, large bowl, medium bowl, cooling rack

1. Preheat the oven to 400 degrees F. Lightly grease a muffin tin, including the top edges.
2. In a large bowl, mix the flour, sugar, baking powder, and salt. Make a well in the center. Set aside.
3. In a medium bowl, beat the egg. Add the milk and oil, and mix until blended. Pour the mixture into the well of dry ingredients and stir until just combined.
4. Add the chocolate chips. Do not overmix.
5. Spoon the batter into the prepared muffin cups, dividing evenly.
6. Bake 20 to 25 minutes, or until the tops are golden and a toothpick inserted in the center comes out clean.
7. Cool muffins in their tin for 5 minutes. Remove the muffins from the tin, cool slightly on a rack, and serve.

Yield: 12 muffins

VARIATIONS

Citrus Zest: *For a mild citrus flavor, add the grated zest of an orange to the batter (step 3).*

Black and Whites: *Use mini chocolate chips or a combination of white and semisweet chocolate chips.*

The First Book of Baking

Cookies

❧ ❧

For bakers who need instant gratification, there is nothing more satisfying than baking a batch of cookies. Since cookies are so easy to prepare and quick to bake, you can usually be munching away, a tall glass of milk at your side, within twenty minutes of first getting the urge.

Some cookie lovers prefer a delicate, buttery shortbread that crumbles and melts in the mouth. Others find nothing rivals the classic—a chewy, morsel-laden chocolate chip cookie. But for many, their craving can be satisfied only with the most decadent cookie of them all, the super-rich fudge brownie. Whatever your preference, you're sure to find a favorite among these classic recipes.

Equipment

Baking Sheets

- Shiny, heavy-gauge aluminum baking sheets with low sides or no sides bake the most evenly.
- If the baking sheets are too thin, the bottoms of the cookies will burn. To prevent burning, double-stack thin baking sheets.

- Insulated baking sheets, which contain a layer of air between two pieces of metal, also prevent burned bottoms. When using this type of "cushioned-air" sheet, it might be necessary to add two to three minutes to the baking time.
- Dark baking sheets absorb more heat and can cause cookie bottoms to burn. When using this type of sheet, reduce the oven temperature twenty-five degrees.
- For proper heat circulation, use baking sheets that allow at least two inches of clearance between your oven walls and the sides of the sheets.
- For accurate baking times, use the pan size specified in the recipes. For simplicity's sake, all bar cookie recipes in this book use a 13 by 9 by 2-inch pan. If necessary, you can substitute two 8 by 8 by 2-inch pans for one 13 by 9 by 2-inch pan, and reduce the minimum baking times by five minutes.

OTHER EQUIPMENT

- Most cookie dough can be mixed easily in a large bowl with a sturdy spoon or your hands.
- Electric mixers are especially helpful for creaming butter and sugar in cookie recipes.
- When using an electric mixer, use caution when adding dry ingredients. Begin mixing on low speed then increase to medium speed for thorough blending. Watch out for flying flour if you add too much at once.
- Some cookie dough is too stiff for handheld mixers, especially when using large amounts of flour. If the mixer becomes strained or overheated, turn it off and stir in the remaining ingredients by hand.
- You can also use a food processor to mix most cookie dough.
- When using an electric mixer or a food processor, make sure to periodically scrape down the sides and bottom of the bowl for better blending.

- Baking cookies on baking sheets lined with parchment is highly recommended. Parchment paper prevents burned cookie bottoms, stops the dough from spreading, and keeps the baking sheets from getting dirty. Parchment paper (available on rolls at most kitchen supply stores) can be wiped down and reused.
- Remove cookies to a cooling rack to prevent burned cookie bottoms.

Ingredients

- Use either bleached or unbleached all-purpose flour.
- Unsalted butter gives cookies a more authentic bakery flavor.
- It is easier to cream butter if it is slightly softened. Butter softened to room temperature (approximately 70 degrees F) will be malleable but should not lose its shape or become oily. Cut the butter into pieces to accelerate the softening process or microwave it for fifteen to twenty seconds.
- Use USDA large eggs at room temperature. To quickly bring eggs to room temperature, place them in very warm water for five to ten minutes.
- Use real, not artificial, chocolate chips.
- Use pure, not imitation, extracts.
- Use unsweetened cocoa powder. To prevent lumps, always stir cocoa before adding it to a batter.

What's in the Cookie Jar?

Drop Cookies

- These easy-to-prepare cookies are formed by dropping mounds of dough directly onto the baking sheet. Depending on the size of the cookie you desire, you can drop dough from a kitchen tablespoon (not a measuring spoon), an ice cream scoop, or a measuring cup. For larger cookies, add three to five minutes to the cooking time.

- For perfectly round cookies, form the dough into even-sized balls by rolling it in your hands before placing it on the baking sheet.
- Drop cookie dough can also be shaped into a cylinder, refrigerated or frozen, and sliced and baked at your convenience. These are officially known as refrigerator cookies.
- Chilling drop cookie dough until firm, for thirty to sixty minutes, helps reduce spreading during baking.

ROLLED COOKIES

- Make sure the rolling pin fits comfortably in your hands. If you don't have a rolling pin, use a wine bottle.
- Wood, Formica, or marble countertops make good rolling surfaces.
- To make rolled cookies less sticky and easier to roll, refrigerate the dough until firm. If the dough seems excessively sticky, work in a little extra flour before chilling. Be careful—too much flour will make cookies tough.
- To make rolling out cookies easy, "pre-roll" the cookie dough: After mixing, while cookie dough is still soft, shape it into a disk, flatten it to one-quarter to one-half inch thick, wrap it in plastic wrap or an airtight plastic bag, and refrigerate. Since cookie dough is rolled between one-eighth and one-quarter inch thick, the rolling will be almost complete.
- Chilled dough should be firm but moist enough to roll easily. If it cracks, it's too cold. Should this happen, let the dough sit at room temperature until firm but workable.
- If time is short, briefly chill the cookie dough in the freezer instead of the refrigerator for about fifteen minutes. Make sure the dough is not too cold to roll.

- To prevent sticking, roll out cookies on a lightly floured surface. Dust flour over the work surface and lightly flour the rolling pin. You can also roll out cookies between sheets of waxed paper (lightly floured, if necessary) or plastic wrap. After rolling, peel off the paper or wrap.
- Roll out small portions of dough at a time. Cover and refrigerate the remainder so it remains firm and moist. Chilled dough also absorbs less flour when it is rolled, so cookies stay more tender.
- Be careful not to overroll the dough or the cookies will be tough. Don't reroll scraps more than once or twice. Instead of rerolling scraps, form them into a log, refrigerate, and use for slice-and-bake cookies.
- Dip cookie-cutter edges in flour to prevent them from sticking to the dough.
- To get the maximum number of cookies when using cookie cutters, start cutting at the outside edge of the rolled dough and work toward the center, cutting the cookies as close to each other as possible.

Bar Cookies

- For easier cleanup, line the baking pan with aluminum foil extended over the edges of the pan. After cooling, gently lift out the foil and the bar cookies together and cut.
- To line baking pans easily, turn the pan upside down and mold a sheet of foil over the outside of the pan. Then flip the pan over and drop the foil inside for a perfect fit. If the recipe calls for a greased pan, lightly spray or grease the foil.
- Spread the dough evenly in the pan, using your fingertips or a spatula, making sure to cover the corners.
- To prevent overcooked sides on bar cookies, use Magi-Cake Strips around the outside of the pan. These aluminized fabric

strips are moistened and placed around the outside of the baking pan. The moisture and insulation from the strips slows down the heat transfer of the metal sides against the batter and prevents edges from drying out.

- For perfectly equal bars, use a ruler to mark cut lines.

Cookin' Cookies

GETTING READY

- Prepare the oven. If you're baking with one pan or sheet, position the oven rack in the middle of the oven. If you're baking with two sheets, position both oven racks near the center of the oven, making sure to leave enough room between the shelves for the heat to circulate.
- Always preheat the oven for at least fifteen minutes before baking.
- Prepare the baking sheets or pans. When a recipe calls for greasing cooking sheets or pans, use a light coating of non-stick vegetable spray, butter, or vegetable shortening. A light coating prevents excess spreading and keeps cookies from sticking. It is not necessary to grease parchment paper.
- Form cookies the same size, shape, and thickness to ensure uniform baking.
- Arrange the cookie dough at equal intervals on the baking sheet. Leave at least two inches between cookies so that they bake evenly and don't spread into each other.

BAKING

- For even baking, rotate baking sheets from front to back, and from top to bottom if using two sheets, midway through the cooking time.

- If you're baking on two sheets at the same time, baking might take a minute or two longer because heat doesn't circulate as freely.
- Cool baking sheets between batches so the dough doesn't start melting before it is set by the oven's heat (a quick method is to run cold water on the back of the sheets). Alternatively, measure and cut parchment paper or aluminum foil the size of your baking sheets and place the dough on the paper or foil while you're waiting for the cookies in the oven to finish. Remove the baked cookies, put the paper or foil with the cookie dough on the baking sheets, and put them directly into the oven.
- Try not to look in the oven too frequently. Opening and shutting the oven door lowers the oven temperature, letting cooler air in and hot air out, and can affect baking times. If you're baking several sheets of cookies in a row, it may be necessary to add a couple of minutes to baking times to compensate for frequent changes in oven temperatures.
- Check the cookies a couple of minutes before the minimum baking time. Watch for changes in color and texture. The dough should lose its shine, darken, and form a light crust.
- A cookie is done when it has spread slightly, is lightly browned, and is slightly firm when touched.
- In general, it is better to underbake cookies and brownies than to overbake them—they will continue to bake when removed from the oven and will harden as they cool.
- For soft and chewy cookies, slightly underbake them. For crispy cookies, add a little time (being careful not to burn bottoms or edges).

COOLING

- Unless noted in the recipe, remove the cookies from the baking sheets and put them on a cooling rack as soon as they have set (usually one to two minutes), so they remain crisp and do not continue cooking from the heat of the sheets.

- Cool bar cookies in their pan, on a cooling rack, before cutting.

STORING

- Cool cookies completely before storing them. Bar cookies can be stored, tightly covered, in their baking pan.
- Do not keep soft and crisp cookies in the same container. Store soft cookies in an airtight container. Store crisp cookies in a container with a loose lid.
- To soften cookies that have hardened, place an apple wedge on a piece of waxed paper in the container with the cookies. Remove the apple after one day and continue to store the cookies tightly sealed.
- When storing delicate or frosted cookies, put waxed paper between layers to keep cookies from sticking together or breaking.
- If cookies or brownies break, mix them into ice cream or frozen yogurt for a delicious treat.
- Most cookie dough can be tightly wrapped and stored in the refrigerator for up to one week, or in the freezer for up to six months before baking. To bake frozen cookie dough, simply slice off half-inch pieces, place on a baking sheet, and add two minutes to the original baking time.
- Baked cookies can be frozen for up to eight months if packed in airtight containers or zip-top bags. Thaw cookies for fifteen to thirty minutes at room temperature. If necessary, re-crisp thawed cookies in a 300-degree-F oven for three to five minutes.
- Thawed cookies can be refrozen.

Chocolate Biscotti

2 cups all-purpose flour
1/3 cup unsweetened cocoa, plus extra for dusting
1 teaspoon baking soda
1/4 teaspoon salt
2 eggs
1 cup granulated sugar
1 teaspoon vanilla extract
1 cup almonds, coarsely chopped

These crisp chocolate biscotti pack a powerful crunch. Close your eyes and imagine that you're enjoying them in an outdoor café in Italy.

Prep Time: 10 to 15 minutes
Baking Time: 55 to 65 minutes, total
Equipment: baking sheets, measuring spoons, measuring cups, medium bowl, large bowl, sturdy spoon, serrated or sharp knife, cooling rack (electric mixer or food processor, optional)

1. Preheat the oven to 350 degrees F. Line 2 baking sheets with parchment paper or foil, shiny side up.
2. In a medium bowl, mix the flour, cocoa, baking soda, and salt. Set aside.
3. In a large bowl, using a sturdy spoon or an electric mixer, lightly beat the eggs, sugar, and vanilla.
4. Gradually add the dry ingredients to the egg mixture. The dough will be dry and crumbly. Mix until the dough begins to take form.
5. Mix in the almonds. The dough will be heavy and sticky.
6. Scrape the dough out onto a work surface lightly coated with cocoa. Lightly coat your hands with cocoa and knead briefly until the dough is soft and not sticky (about 8 to 10 times). Divide the dough into 2 pieces.
7. Shape each piece into a log about 10 inches long, 2 inches wide, and 1 inch high. Carefully transfer the logs to a baking sheet, placing them 4 inches apart.
8. Bake for 35 to 40 minutes, or until well risen and very firm to the touch. Remove from the oven and reduce the temperature to 325 degrees F.

(Continues)

9. Cool the cylinders on a baking sheet for 10 minutes, until warm but not too hot to touch. Peel off the paper or foil and transfer the logs to a cutting board.
10. Using a serrated or sharp knife, cut the biscotti diagonally into $\frac{1}{2}$-inch slices. Use a firm and fast cutting motion to prevent crumbling.
11. Lay the biscotti flat on the baking sheets. You will need 2 sheets to fit all of the biscotti. Bake until firm and very dry, about 20 to 25 minutes. The cookies might be slightly soft in the center but will harden as they cool.
12. Let the biscotti stand on the baking sheet for 2 minutes, then cool them on a rack. Cool biscotti completely before storing or they may become soggy.

Yield: Approximately 40 biscotti

VARIATIONS

Chocolate-Coated Biscotti: *After baking, spread the bottom half of the biscotti with melted dark or white chocolate, or drizzle chocolate over the entire cookie. Lay the cookie on waxed paper until dry.*

Chocolate-Nut Dipped Biscotti: *After baking, dip the sides of the biscotti in melted chocolate and roll them in 1 cup of finely chopped nuts.*

Chocolate–Chocolate Chip Biscotti: *Add 1 cup mini chocolate chips to the batter (step 5).*

A Hint of Something: *For gentle flavoring, add either 2 teaspoons instant espresso or coffee powder or 2 teaspoons grated orange zest to the batter (step 4).*

Kneading biscotti in cocoa powder, instead of flour, gives a slight choco-late boost and is a better color match.

Use either blanched or unblanched almonds. To blanch almonds, place them in boiling water for one minute, then rinse in cold water. The skins will peel right off. Let the almonds dry completely before using.

For richer almond flavor, lightly toast the nuts on a baking sheet at 350 degrees F for eight to ten minutes, until aromatic and golden, or substi-tute almond extract for vanilla.

Biscotti can also be made in a food processor fitted with a metal chop-ping blade. Mix the eggs and vanilla first, then add the dry ingredients.

Biscotti dough might be too heavy for a handheld mixer. For easier mix-ing, use a standing mixer with a paddle attachment, a food processor, or mix by hand.

For extra-wide biscotti, shape the dough into a single fourteen-inch-long roll and flatten to one inch thick.

To keep biscotti from crumbling when slicing, hold the log near the end being sliced, exerting gentle pressure on the top. If it is still crumbling, return it to the oven for another five minutes.

To ensure extra-crisp biscotti, turn the cookies over halfway through the second baking.

For softer biscotti, keep them in a closed paper bag for a day or two.

To recrisp biscotti, bake them in a 350-degree-F oven for ten minutes.

Blondies

2½ cups all-purpose flour
2 teaspoons baking
    powder
½ teaspoon salt
1 cup (2 sticks) butter,
    melted
1½ cups brown sugar, firmly
    packed
2 teaspoons vanilla extract
3 eggs
2 cups semisweet
    chocolate chips

Also known as butterscotch brownies, these chocolate chip bars are a thicker, more cake-like version of chocolate chip cookies. Try them for something a little different.

Prep Time: 5 to 10 minutes
Baking Time: 25 to 30 minutes
Equipment: 13 by 9 by 2-inch baking pan, measuring spoons, measuring cups, medium bowl, large bowl, sturdy spoon, spatula, cooling rack (electric mixer or food processor, optional)

1. Preheat the oven to 350 degrees F. Lightly grease a 13 by 9 by 2-inch baking pan.
2. In a medium bowl, mix the flour, baking powder, and salt. Set aside.
3. In a large bowl, using a sturdy spoon or an electric mixer, combine the butter, brown sugar, and vanilla.
4. Add the eggs and beat until thoroughly combined.
5. Gradually add the dry ingredients and mix well.
6. Stir in the chocolate chips.
7. Pour the batter into the prepared pan. Smooth the top with a spatula.
8. Bake 25 to 30 minutes, or until golden and a toothpick inserted in the center comes out almost clean. The blondies will still be slightly moist in the center, but should bounce back when touched.
9. Cool completely on a rack before cutting.

Yield: Approximately 36 blondies

Incredibly Nutty Blondies: *Mix 1 cup chopped nuts into the batter (step 6), and sprinkle $^1/_2$ cup chopped nuts on top before baking.*

Lots of Chips Blondies: *Use a combination of semisweet chocolate, milk chocolate, butterscotch, and white chocolate chips.*

Maple-Walnut Blondies: *Add $^1/_2$ cup maple syrup to the batter (step 4), and substitute chopped walnuts for the chocolate chips (step 6).*

TIPS

The secret for sensational blondies is to slightly underbake them. This gives them their dense, chewy texture. If you prefer a more cake-like blondie, bake for an additional three to five minutes, or until a toothpick inserted in the center comes out dry.

For easier cleanup, line the pan with aluminum foil, leaving a one-inch overhang, before pouring in the batter. After cooling, lift the foil and the blondies out of the pan together.

Use Magi-Cake Strips around the pan to keep the edges from overcooking.

If the edges dry out, trim and use them as mix-ins for ice cream or frozen yogurt.

Brownies

❧ ☙

1¼ cups all-purpose flour
½ teaspoon baking powder
¼ teaspoon salt
1 cup (2 sticks) butter, melted
2 cups granulated sugar
1 tablespoon vanilla extract
3 eggs
¾ cup unsweetened cocoa
1½ cups semisweet chocolate chips

In the battle for the ultimate brownies, there is no match for these dense, rich, fudge-like creations. A warning to chocoholics: These brownies are intoxicating. Eat at your own risk.

Prep Time: 5 to 10 minutes
Baking Time: 30 to 35 minutes
Equipment: 13 by 9 by 2-inch baking pan, measuring spoons, measuring cups, medium bowl, large bowl, sturdy spoon, spatula, cooling rack (electric mixer or food processor, optional)

1. Preheat the oven to 350 degrees F. Lightly grease a 13 by 9 by 2-inch baking pan.
2. In a medium bowl, mix the flour, baking powder, and salt. Set aside.
3. In a large bowl, using a sturdy spoon or an electric mixer, combine the butter, sugar, and vanilla.
4. Add the eggs and beat until well blended.
5. Add the cocoa and beat until thoroughly combined.
6. Gradually add the dry ingredients and mix well.
7. Stir in 1 cup of the chocolate chips, reserving the rest for the next step.
8. Pour the batter into the prepared pan. Smooth the top with a spatula. Sprinkle the remaining ½ cup of chips on top.
9. Bake 30 to 35 minutes, or until a toothpick inserted in the center comes out almost clean. The brownies will still be slightly moist in the center, but should bounce back when touched.
10. Cool completely on a rack before cutting.

Yield: Approximately 36 brownies

Incredibly Nutty Brownies: *Mix 1 cup chopped nuts into the batter (step 7), and sprinkle $1/2$ cup chopped nuts on top before baking.*

Triple-Chip Brownies: *Use a combination of semisweet chocolate, milk chocolate, and white chocolate chips for an especially festive presentation.*

Peanut Butter Cup Brownies: *Replace the chocolate chips with peanut butter chips, and top with $1/2$ cup chopped peanut butter cups.*

TIPS

The secret for sensational brownies is to slightly underbake them. This gives them their dense, fudgy texture. If you prefer a more cake-like brownie, bake for an additional three to five minutes, or until a toothpick inserted in the center comes out dry.

For easier cleanup, line the pan with aluminum foil, leaving a one-inch overhang, before pouring in the batter. After cooling, lift the foil and the brownies out of the pan together.

Use Magi-Cake Strips around the pan to keep the edges from overcooking.

If the edges dry out, trim and use them as mix-ins for ice cream or frozen yogurt.

Butter Cookies

ॐ ॐ

1 cup (2 sticks) unsalted
butter, softened
¾ cup granulated sugar
1 teaspoon vanilla extract
1 egg
2¼ cups all-purpose flour
¼ teaspoon salt
½ cup granulated sugar
(for coating)

These delicate and tender butter cookies melt in your mouth. Pipe them from a pastry bag for an extra-special look.

Prep Time: 10 to 15 minutes
Baking Time: 10 to 15 minutes
Equipment: baking sheets, measuring spoons, measuring cups, large bowl, sturdy spoon, cooling rack (electric mixer or food processor, optional)

1. Preheat the oven to 375 degrees F. Take out the baking sheets.
2. In a large bowl, using a sturdy spoon or an electric mixer, cream the butter until fluffy and lightened in color.
3. Add the sugar and beat until well blended.
4. Add the vanilla and the egg. Beat until thoroughly combined.
5. Gradually add the flour and salt and mix well. The dough will be dry and crumbly at first but will come together. Do not overmix.
6. If time allows, refrigerate the dough for an hour to make it easier to handle.
7. Shape the dough into balls 1½ inches in diameter. Roll each ball in sugar to coat. Gently flatten the cookies until they measure about 2½ inches. Place them 2 inches apart on the ungreased baking sheets.
8. Bake 10 to 15 minutes, or until the cookies are golden and edges are lightly browned.
9. Let the cookies stand for 1 minute before transferring them to a cooling rack.

Yield: Approximately 48 cookies (depending on size of cookies)

Chips Galore: *Add 1 cup mini chocolate chips to batter (step 5).*

Chocolate-Coated Cookies: *After baking, dip the sides or bottom of the cookies into melted chocolate.*

Thumbprint Cookies: *After you flatten the cookies, make an indentation in the center with your thumb. Fill it with raspberry preserves or a jam of your choice (make sure the jam is firm or it will run and stain the cookie). To ensure the best presentation, cook the jam until concentrated and place it in the center of the cookie after baking.*

Sugar and Spice: *Roll the cookie balls in mixture of 3 tablespoons sugar and 1 teaspoon cinnamon (step 7).*

TIPS

If you don't have unsalted butter, you may use salted butter but the flavor will be less authentic. Do not substitute margarine.

For richer flavor, substitute two egg yolks for the egg.

These cookies can also be mixed in a food processor fitted with a metal chopping blade.

If you refrigerate the dough before baking, wait to preheat the oven until fifteen minutes before you are ready to bake.

For an interesting design, flatten the cookies with the bottom of a decorated glass that has been buttered and dipped in sugar.

For "spritz" cookies, pipe the cookie dough with a pastry bag fitted with a large rosette or star attachment. Place the bag directly over the baking sheet and firmly squeeze the bag until the cookies are about two inches in diameter. Then stop squeezing and lift the tube straight up and away. For the best presentation, place melted chocolate, a chocolate chip, or a candied cherry in the middle of each cookie before baking. Do not refrigerate the dough before piping or it will be too stiff.

For giant cookies, use a quarter-cup measuring cup and drop the dough four inches apart. Add approximately three minutes to the baking time.

Gingersnaps

꿍ᦠ ᦣꙷ

2¼ cups all-purpose flour
2 teaspoons baking soda
½ teaspoon salt
1 tablespoon ground
   ginger
1 teaspoon ground
   cinnamon
½ teaspoon ground black
   pepper
½ teaspoon ground allspice
¾ cup (1½ sticks) butter,
   softened
1 cup brown sugar, firmly
   packed
1 egg
¼ cup molasses
½ cup granulated sugar
   (for coating)

These fragrant gems are wonderful with a cup of tea or a tall glass of milk. The surprising addition of pepper adds to their spiciness.

Prep Time: 10 to 15 minutes, plus 1 hour to chill
Baking Time: 12 to 16 minutes
Equipment: baking sheets, measuring spoons, measuring cups, medium bowl, large bowl, sturdy spoon, cooling rack (electric mixer or food processor, optional)

1. In a medium bowl, mix the flour, baking soda, salt, ginger, cinnamon, black pepper, and allspice. Set aside.
2. In a large bowl, using a sturdy spoon or an electric mixer, cream the butter until fluffy and lightened in color.
3. Add the brown sugar and beat until well blended.
4. Add the egg and molasses. Beat until thoroughly combined.
5. Gradually add the dry ingredients and mix well. The dough will be sticky.
6. Refrigerate the dough for 1 hour to make it easier to handle.
7. Preheat the oven to 350 degrees F, 15 minutes before dough is ready. Take out the baking sheets.
8. Shape the dough into balls 1½ inches in diameter. Dip the tops in granulated sugar. Place the balls, sugared side up, about 2 inches apart on the ungreased baking sheets.

9. Bake 12 to 16 minutes, or until the cookies are firm to the touch and the edges are beginning to brown.
10. Let the cookies stand for 1 minute before transfering them to a cooling rack.

Yield: Approximately 48 cookies (depending on size of cookies)

VARIATION

Double Ginger: *Add 1 tablespoon finely chopped crystallized ginger to the dry ingredients for extra ginger flavor (step 1).*

TIPS

These cookies can also be mixed in a food processor fitted with a metal chopping blade.

For giant cookies, use a one-quarter-cup measuring cup and drop the dough four inches apart. Add approximately three minutes to the baking time.

Toffee Bars

These layered bars have a golden toffee-like crust and a thick layer of chocolate and nuts on top.

1	cup (2 sticks) butter, softened
1	cup light brown sugar, firmly packed
1	egg yolk
2	teaspoons vanilla extract
2	cups all-purpose flour
¼	teaspoon salt
2	cups semisweet chocolate chips
1	cup walnuts, coarsely chopped

Prep Time: 5 to 10 minutes
Baking Time: 28 to 34 minutes, total
Equipment: 13 by 9 by 2-inch baking pan, measuring spoons, measuring cups, large bowl, sturdy spoon, cooling rack (electric mixer or food processor, optional)

1. Preheat the oven to 350 degrees F. Lightly grease a 13 by 9 by 2-inch baking pan.
2. In a large bowl, using a sturdy spoon or an electric mixer, cream the butter and sugar until fluffy and lightened in color.
3. Add the egg yolk and vanilla and beat until well blended.
4. Gradually add the flour and salt and mix until thoroughly combined. The mixture will be crumbly at first but will come together.
5. Pat the dough evenly into the pan. The dough will be thick and sticky.
6. Bake for 25 to 30 minutes, or until the top is golden brown and firm to the touch.
7. Remove the toffee bars from the oven and distribute the chocolate chips evenly over the top.
8. Return the bars to the oven for 3 to 4 minutes, or until the chocolate melts. The chips will not lose their shape but will be shiny.

The First Book of Baking

9. Remove the bars from the oven and spread the chocolate evenly. Sprinkle with nuts.
10. Cool the toffee bars completely on a rack before cutting.

Yield: Approximately 36 bars

VARIATION

Lots-of-Toffee Bars: *Add 1 cup crushed toffee pieces to the walnuts and sprinkle on top of the melted chocolate (step 9).*

TIPS

For easier cleanup, line the pan with aluminum foil, leaving a one-inch overhang, before adding the dough. After cooling, lift the foil and the toffee bars out of the pan together.

Chocolate Chip Cookies

2¼ cups all-purpose flour
1 teaspoon baking soda
½ teaspoon salt
1 cup (2 sticks) butter, softened
¾ cup granulated sugar
¾ cup brown sugar, firmly packed
1 teaspoon vanilla extract
2 eggs
2 cups semisweet chocolate chips or chocolate chunks
1 cup walnuts, chopped (optional)

The king of all cookies had humble origins. In 1933 Ruth Graves Wakefield at the Tollhouse Inn didn't have time to melt the chocolate before baking her cookies. She presumed if she used chocolate chunks they'd melt while baking and save her some time. Instead, a star was born.

Prep Time: 5 to 10 minutes
Baking Time: 8 to 12 minutes
Equipment: baking sheets, measuring spoons, measuring cups, medium bowl, large bowl, sturdy spoon, cooling rack (electric mixer or food processor, optional)

1. Preheat the oven to 375 degrees F. Take out the baking sheets.
2. In a medium bowl, mix the flour, baking soda, and salt. Set aside.
3. In a large bowl, using a sturdy spoon or an electric mixer, cream the butter until fluffy and lightened in color.
4. Add both sugars and beat until well blended.
5. Add the vanilla and eggs. Beat until thoroughly combined.
6. Gradually add the dry ingredients and mix well.
7. Stir in the chocolate chips and walnuts.
8. If time allows, refrigerate the dough until firm to prevent excess spreading, about 30 minutes.
9. Drop the dough by rounded tablespoons, 2 inches apart, onto the ungreased baking sheets.

10. Bake 8 to 12 minutes, or until the cookies are golden and the edges are lightly browned.
11. Let the cookies stand for 1 minute before transferring them to a cooling rack.

Yield: Approximately 48 cookies (depending on size of cookies)

VARIATIONS

Chips Galore: *Substitute white chocolate, milk chocolate, peanut butter, or butterscotch chips, or a combination, for the semisweet chips.*

Candy Cookies: *Substitute candy-coated milk chocolate pieces (such as M&Ms), chopped malted milk balls, or toffee bits for some or all of the chips.*

Upscale Chippers: *Replace the semisweet chips with white chocolate chips or chunks, and substitute chopped macadamia nuts for walnuts.*

Ice Cream Sandwiches: *Spread softened ice cream between two large cookies for a wonderful summertime treat. Freeze until ready to use.*

TIPS

These cookies can also be mixed in a food processor fitted with a metal chopping blade.

If you refrigerate the dough before baking, wait to preheat the oven until fifteen minutes before you are ready to bake.

For "gourmet" looking (and tasting) cookies, substitute twelve ounces of chopped chocolate from a high-quality semisweet or bittersweet chocolate bar for the semisweet chips.

For giant cookies, use a one-quarter-cup measuring cup and drop the dough four inches apart. Add approximately three minutes to the baking time.

Ranger Granger Cookies

2¼ cups all-purpose flour
1 teaspoon baking soda
½ teaspoon salt
1 cup (2 sticks) butter, softened
¾ cup granulated sugar
¾ cup brown sugar, firmly packed
1 teaspoon vanilla extract
2 eggs
1 cup uncooked oatmeal
1 cup shredded sweetened coconut
2 cups semisweet chocolate chips or chocolate chunks
1 cup walnuts, chopped

A campground favorite, these yummy cookies have a little bit of everything . . . chocolate chips, coconut, oatmeal, and walnuts!

Prep Time: 10 to 15 minutes
Baking Time: 8 to 12 minutes
Equipment: baking sheets, measuring spoons, measuring cups, medium bowl, large bowl, sturdy spoon, cooling rack (electric mixer or food processor, optional)

1. Preheat the oven to 375 degrees F. Take out the baking sheets.
2. In a medium bowl, mix the flour, baking soda, and salt. Set aside.
3. In a large bowl, using a sturdy spoon or an electric mixer, cream the butter until fluffy and lightened in color.
4. Add both sugars and beat until well blended.
5. Add the vanilla and eggs. Beat until thoroughly combined.
6. Gradually add the dry ingredients and mix well.
7. Mix in the oatmeal and coconut until blended.
8. Stir in the chocolate chips and walnuts.
9. If time allows, refrigerate the dough until firm to prevent excess spreading, about 30 minutes.
10. Drop the dough by rounded tablespoons, 2 inches apart, onto the ungreased baking sheets.

The First Book of Baking

11. Bake 8 to 12 minutes, or until the cookies are golden and the edges are lightly browned.
12. Let the cookies stand for 1 minute before transferring them to a cooling rack.

Yield: Approximately 48 cookies (depending on size of cookies)

VARIATIONS

Chips Galore: *Use white chocolate, milk chocolate, peanut butter, or butterscotch chips for variety.*

Raisin Grangers: *Add $1/2$ cup raisins with the chocolate chips.*

Go Nutty: *Substitute pecans, peanuts, or macadamia nuts for the walnuts.*

TIPS

These cookies can also be mixed in a food processor fitted with a metal chopping blade.

If you refrigerate the dough before baking, wait to preheat the oven until fifteen minutes before you are ready to bake.

For giant cookies, use a one-quarter-cup measuring cup and drop the dough four inches apart. Add approximately three minutes to the baking time.

Cream Cheese Brownies

Brownies

1   cup (2 sticks) butter, cut into large pieces
2   cups semisweet choco-late chips
3   eggs
1   cup granulated sugar
1   cup all-purpose flour
1   teaspoon baking powder
2   teaspoons vanilla extract

Cream Cheese Topping

8   ounces cream cheese, softened
3   tablespoons butter, softened
1   teaspoon vanilla extract
½   cup granulated sugar
2   eggs

These brownies are made with melted chocolate and topped with a marbleized cream cheese mixture. They look so elegant, it's hard to believe how easy they are to make.

Prep Time: 10 to 15 minutes
Baking Time: 30 to 35 minutes
Equipment: 13 by 9 by 2-inch baking pan, measuring spoons, measuring cups, large bowl, sturdy spoon, medium bowl, spatula or knife, cooling rack (electric mixer or food processor, optional)

1. Preheat the oven to 350 degrees F. Lightly grease a 13 by 9 by 2-inch baking pan.
2. Prepare the brownies. Melt the butter and chocolate. Set aside to cool.
3. In a large bowl, using a sturdy spoon or an electric mixer, beat the eggs and sugar until thick and pale yellow.
4. Add the flour, baking powder, and vanilla, and mix thoroughly.
5. Stir in the melted chocolate mixture.
6. Spread two-thirds of the brownie batter into the prepared pan, making sure to distribute the batter evenly, especially into the corners. It will just cover the pan. Set aside.
7. Prepare the cream cheese topping. In a medium bowl, beat the cream cheese, butter, vanilla, and sugar together until soft and fluffy, making sure to scrape the beaters, sides, and bottom of the mixing bowl.
8. Add the eggs and beat well. The mixture will be quite liquid.
9. Pour the cream cheese mixture on top of the brownie batter. Gently shake the pan to distribute evenly.

10. Drop spoonfuls of the reserved brownie batter on the cream cheese mixture every 1 to 2 inches.
11. Using a spatula or knife, gently swirl the brownie batter and the cream cheese mixture to create a marbleized design. Don't overdo it.
12. Bake 30 to 35 minutes, or until a toothpick inserted in the center comes out almost clean. The brownies will still be slightly moist in the center, but should bounce back when touched.
13. Cool completely on a rack before cutting.

Yield: Approximately 36 brownies

VARIATIONS

Lots-of-Chips Brownies: *Add $^1/_2$ cup mini chocolate chips to the cream cheese mixture (step 8).*

Peanut Butter Marble: *Mix $^3/_4$ cup peanut butter into the cream cheese mixture (step 8).*

TIPS

The secret for sensational brownies is to slightly underbake them. This gives them their dense, chewy texture. If you prefer a more cake-like brownie, bake for an additional three to five minutes, or until a toothpick inserted in the center comes out dry.

For easier cleanup, line the pan with aluminum foil, leaving a one-inch overhang, before pouring in the batter. After cooling, lift the foil and the brownies out of the pan together.

Use Magi-Cake Strips around the pan to keep the edges from overcooking.

If you have cocoa on hand but no chocolate chips, use the basic Brownie recipe on page 60.

If the edges dry out, trim and use them as mix-ins for ice cream or frozen yogurt.

Macaroons

1/3 cup all-purpose flour
2¾ cups (approximately 8 ounces) shredded sweetened coconut
⅛ teaspoon salt
⅔ cup (7 ounces) sweetened condensed milk (not evaporated milk)
1 teaspoon vanilla extract

There are many different versions of macaroons and many ways to prepare them. These chewy coconut macaroons are both delicious and easy to make!

Prep Time: 5 to 10 minutes
Baking Time: 13 to 18 minutes
Equipment: baking sheet, measuring spoons, measuring cups, large bowl, cooling rack

1. Preheat the oven to 350 degrees F. Grease a baking sheet well.
2. In a large bowl, mix the flour, coconut, and salt.
3. Add the condensed milk and vanilla, and stir well. The batter will be thick and sticky.
4. Shape the dough into 2-inch balls, or drop generous tablespoons onto the baking sheet about 2 inches apart.
5. Bake 13 to 18 minutes, or until the macaroons are golden and firm to the touch.
6. Remove the macaroons from the baking sheet immediately to prevent sticking, and cool on a rack.

Yield: Approximately 12 macaroons

VARIATIONS

Chocolate Macaroons: *Add 1 ounce melted unsweetened chocolate to the condensed milk (step 3), or add 3 tablespoons unsweetened cocoa to the dry ingredients (step 2).*

Nutty Macaroons: *Add ½ cup chopped toasted almonds to the dry ingredients (step 2).*

Chocolate-Coated Macaroons: *After baking, spread the bottom half of each macaroon with melted chocolate, or drizzle chocolate over the entire cookie. Lay the cookies on waxed paper until dry and set.*

Chocolate Chip Macaroons: *Add $^1/_2$ cup mini chocolate chips to the batter (step 3).*

TIPS

For easier cleanup, line the baking sheets with parchment paper or greased aluminum foil.

Check the cookies for burning bottoms during baking. Use insulated baking sheets, or double-stack for better protection.

Gingerbread People

Cookies

2 1/2 cups all-purpose flour
1/2 teaspoon salt
1 teaspoon baking soda
2 teaspoons ground cinnamon
2 teaspoons ground ginger
1 teaspoon ground cloves
1/2 cup (1 stick) butter, softened
1/2 cup brown sugar, firmly packed
1 egg
1/2 cup molasses

Frosting (optional)

3 cups confectioners' sugar
2 to 3 tablespoons milk, plus additional milk
Food coloring (optional)

Gingerbread figures are fun to prepare for old and young alike. Their aroma alone will tell you it's holiday time.

Prep Time: 15 to 20 minutes, plus an hour or more to chill
Baking Time: 8 to 13 minutes
Equipment: baking sheets, measuring spoons, measuring cups, medium bowl, large bowl, sturdy spoon, rolling pin, cookie cutters or sharp knife, cooling rack (electric mixer or food processor, pastry bag, small spatula or brush, optional)

1. In a medium bowl, mix the flour, salt, baking soda, cinnamon, ginger, and cloves. Set aside.
2. In a large bowl, using a sturdy spoon or an electric mixer, cream the butter until fluffy and lightened in color.
3. Add the brown sugar and beat until well blended.
4. Add the egg and molasses. Beat until thoroughly combined.
5. Gradually add the dry ingredients and mix well.
6. Scrape the dough onto a sheet of plastic wrap. It will be soft and sticky. Press the dough together to form a flat disk between 1/4 and 1/2 inch thick. Wrap tightly and refrigerate until firm, 1 to 2 hours.
7. When the cookies are ready to roll out, preheat the oven to 350 degrees F. Take out the baking sheets.
8. On a lightly floured surface, with a lightly floured rolling pin, roll out the dough 1/8 to 1/4 inch thick, lifting and turning it frequently to prevent sticking (add additional flour if necessary to prevent sticking). With flour-dipped cookie cutters or a sharp knife, cut the dough into desired shapes. Carefully transfer the dough to ungreased baking sheets.

The First Book of Baking

9. Bake 8 to 13 minutes, or until the cookies are firm to the touch and the edges are beginning to brown.
10. Let the cookies stand for 1 minute before transferring them to a cooling rack. Cool completely before frosting.
11. Frost the cookies (optional). In a small bowl, combine the confectioners' sugar and milk. Mix until smooth and creamy, but stiff enough that the frosting does not flow from a spoon (if necessary, add additional milk or sugar, $1/2$ teaspoon at a time, to reach the desired consistency). Use a pastry bag with a small rounded tip (or fill a zip-top plastic bag with icing and cut off the bottom corner) to pipe decorations. To glaze cookies, add additional milk, $1/2$ teaspoon at a time, until the mixture flows from a spoon. For colored icing or glaze, divide the frosting into small bowls and add food coloring, a few drops at a time. Spread the icing or glaze with a small spatula or brush. If you are piping frosting on top of a glaze, wait for the glaze to dry first. Allow the decorated cookies to dry completely before storing (about 2 hours).

Yield: Approximately 36 cookies (depending on size of cookies)

VARIATIONS

Decorated Gingerbread People: *Frost the cookies, and use candies or raisins for eyes, mouths, or buttons. Add the decorations before the glaze dries. Allow cookies to dry completely before storing (about 2 hours).*

TIPS

These cookies can also be mixed in a food processor fitted with a metal chopping blade.

A ruler is handy for measuring the thickness of rolled-out dough.

If you don't have cookie cutters in the shape you want, make patterns out of cardboard and cut around them.

If you want to hang cookies from the Christmas tree, make a small hole in the dough before baking.

To prevent the dough from being too sticky to roll out, refrigerate it until firm. If the dough seems excessively sticky after mixing, work in a little extra flour before chilling.

Chilled dough should be moist enough to roll easily. It should not crack when rolled. If the dough is too cold, let it sit at room temperature until firm but workable. If the dough becomes sticky during rolling, add flour to your rolling surface and rolling pin.

Cookies can be rolled out on a lightly floured surface or rolled between sheets of waxed paper or plastic wrap (lightly flour first, if necessary). Be careful not to overwork the dough, or the cookies will be tough. Roll out small portions of dough at a time, refrigerating the remainder so it remains firm. Don't reroll scraps more than once or twice, or the cookies will be tough (chill first if necessary).

Do not roll the dough too thin—one-quarter-inch-thick dough is easy to work with and resists tears.

Beginning cookie makers should avoid cookie cutters with very intricate designs. The dough will be more difficult to transfer from the cutter to the baking sheets.

Set up a design center with cookie cutters, candies, frosting, and other decorations. Line the work surface with waxed paper or foil for easier cleanup.

Combine decorating techniques. Glaze cookies and then pipe or drizzle with different colored icing or add raisins or candies.

Cookies do not have to be rolled out. You can also form them into one-and-a-half-inch balls, flatten to one-quarter inch thick, and bake.

Biscotti

2 cups all-purpose flour
1 teaspoon baking powder
½ teaspoon baking soda
¼ teaspoon salt
2 eggs
1 cup granulated sugar
1 teaspoon vanilla extract
1 cup almonds, coarsely
    chopped

In Italian, the word biscotti *means both "cookies" and "twice baked." What apt descriptions for these crisp delights, which are wonderful dipped in coffee or wine.*

Prep Time: 10 to 15 minutes
Baking Time: 55 to 65 minutes, total
Equipment: baking sheets, measuring spoons, measuring cups, medium bowl, large bowl, sturdy spoon, serrated or sharp knife, cooling rack (electric mixer or food processor, optional)

1. Preheat the oven to 350 degrees F. Line 2 baking sheets with parchment paper or foil, shiny side up.
2. In a medium bowl, mix the flour, baking powder, baking soda, and salt. Set aside.
3. In a large bowl, using a sturdy spoon or an electric mixer, lightly beat the eggs, sugar, and vanilla.
4. Gradually add the dry ingredients to the egg mixture. The dough will be dry and crumbly. Mix until the dough begins to take form.
5. Mix in the almonds. The dough will be thick.
6. Scrape the dough out onto a work surface lightly coated with flour. Lightly coat your hands with flour and knead briefly until the dough is soft and not sticky (about 8 to 10 times). Divide the dough into 2 pieces.
7. Shape each piece into a log about 10 inches long, 2 inches wide, and 1 inch high. Carefully transfer the logs to a baking sheet, placing them 4 inches apart.

(Continues)

Cookies

8. Bake for 35 to 40 minutes, or until well risen, lightly browned, and very firm to the touch. Remove from the oven and reduce the temperature to 325 degrees F.

9. Cool the cylinders on the baking sheet for 10 minutes, until warm but not too hot to touch. Peel off the paper or foil and transfer the logs to a cutting board.

10. Using a serrated or sharp knife, cut the biscotti diagonally into ½-inch slices. Use a firm and fast cutting motion to prevent crumbling.

11. Lay the biscotti flat on the baking sheets. You will need 2 sheets to fit all of the biscotti. Bake until golden, firm, and very dry, 20 to 25 minutes. The cookies might be slightly soft in the center but will harden as they cool.

12. Let the biscotti stand on the baking sheet for 2 minutes, then cool them on a rack. Cool the biscotti completely before storing or they may become soggy.

Yield: Approximately 40 biscotti

VARIATIONS

Chocolate-Coated Biscotti: *After baking, spread the bottom half of the biscotti with melted dark or white chocolate, or drizzle chocolate over the entire cookie. Lay the cookie on waxed paper until dry.*

Chocolate-Nut Dipped Biscotti: *After baking, dip the sides of the biscotti in melted chocolate and roll them in 1 cup of finely chopped nuts.*

A Hint of Something: *For gentle flavoring, add one of the following to the batter in step 4: 2 teaspoons ground anise seed, ¹/₂ teaspoon almond extract, 1 teaspoon cinnamon, 2 teaspoons grated lemon zest, 1 tablespoon grated orange zest, 2 tablespoons minced crystallized ginger.*

Chocolate Chip Biscotti: *Add 1 cup mini chocolate chips to the batter (step 5).*

Fruity Biscotti: *Add 1 cup chopped dried fruit to the batter (step 5).*

The First Book of Baking

Use either blanched or unblanched almonds. To blanch almonds, place them in boiling water for one minute, then rinse in cold water. The skins will peel right off. Let the almonds dry completely before using.

For richer almond flavor, lightly toast the nuts on a baking sheet at 350 degrees F for eight to ten minutes, until aromatic and golden, or substitute almond extract for vanilla.

Biscotti can also be made in a food processor fitted with a metal chopping blade. Mix the eggs and vanilla first, then add the dry ingredients.

Biscotti dough might be too heavy for a handheld mixer. For easier mixing, use a standing mixer with a paddle attachment, a food processor, or mix by hand.

For extra-wide biscotti, shape the dough into a single fourteen-inch-long roll and flatten to one inch thick.

To keep biscotti from crumbling when slicing, hold the log near the end being sliced, exerting gentle pressure on the top. If it is still crumbling, return it to the oven for another five minutes.

To ensure extra-crisp biscotti, turn the cookies over halfway through the second baking.

For softer biscotti, keep them in a closed paper bag for a day or two.

To recrisp biscotti, bake them in a 350-degree-F oven for ten minutes.

Lace Cookies

5 tablespoons butter
⅓ cup all-purpose flour
1 cup uncooked oatmeal (preferably quick-cooking)
½ cup granulated sugar
⅛ teaspoon salt
2 tablespoons molasses
2 tablespoons milk
1 teaspoon vanilla extract
1 cup semisweet chocolate chips

Make these elegant cookies when you want to impress some-one. Sandwiched with chocolate, they are both beautiful and delicious.

Prep Time: 15 to 20 minutes
Baking Time: 5 to 8 minutes
Equipment: baking sheets, measuring spoons, measuring cups, medium saucepan, aluminum foil

1. Preheat the oven to 375 degrees F. Line the baking sheets with aluminum foil.
2. In a medium saucepan, melt the butter over low heat, making sure not to brown it. Remove the pan from the heat and set aside.
3. Add the flour, oatmeal, sugar, salt, molasses, milk, and vanilla to the butter. Mix well. The batter will be caramel colored and pasty.
4. Drop ½ teaspoons of batter, about 4 inches apart, onto foil-covered sheets. Using the back of the spoon, smear the batter thinly on the foil until the cookies are about 2 inches wide. The thinness will give the lacy texture.
5. Bake 5 to 8 minutes, or until the cookies are bubbly, lacy, and deeply golden.

6. Cool 15 minutes or until hardened. Carefully peel the cookies from the foil.
7. Meanwhile, melt the chocolate. Spread the melted chocolate on the flat side of the cookies and sandwich together. The cookies will be irregularly shaped.

Yield: Approximately 20 sandwich cookies

VARIATION

Chocolate-Coated Lace Cookies: *Instead of sandwiching the cookies, spread melted chocolate on the bottom or on half of the cookie. Place the cookies on waxed paper until dry.*

TIPS

If cookies are still soft after cooling and are difficult to peel from the foil, return them to the oven for another minute, take them out, and cool again.

When peeling cookies off the foil, start with thickest part of the cookie to prevent breakage.

These cookies can get soggy if left out too long. Tightly seal and store in the refrigerator or freezer so they keep their crunch.

Lemon Bars

Shortbread Crust

$\frac{1}{4}$ $\frac{1}{2}$ 1   cup (2 sticks) butter,
     softened

½stick 1stick

½   cup confectioners' sugar

2   cups all-purpose flour

Lemon Topping

4   eggs

2   cups granulated sugar

¼   cup all-purpose flour

2   tablespoons lemon zest, grated

6   tablespoons fresh lemon juice

1   teaspoon baking powder

3   tablespoons confectioners' sugar (for sprinkling)

What could be more heavenly than a layer of buttery shortbread topped with a tangy lemon curd? Try these exquisite bars and you'll be singing their praises!

Prep Time: 15 to 20 minutes
Baking Time: 40 to 50 minutes, total
Equipment: 13 by 9 by 2-inch baking pan, measuring spoons, measuring cups, grater, 2 large bowls, whisk, knife, cooling rack, strainer (electric mixer or food processor, optional)

1. Preheat the oven to 350 degrees F. Take out a 13 by 9 by 2-inch baking pan.
2. Prepare the crust. In a large bowl, use your fingertips to combine the butter, confectioners' sugar, and flour until crumbly.
3. Pat the dough evenly into the ungreased baking pan.
4. Bake for 20 to 25 minutes, or until the top is pale golden and firm to the touch.
5. Meanwhile, prepare the topping. In a large bowl, using a whisk or an electric mixer, beat the eggs. Add the sugar, flour, lemon zest, lemon juice, and baking powder, and mix until thoroughly combined.
6. When the crust is ready, remove it from the oven. Pour the lemon mixture over the hot crust.
7. Return the lemon bars to the oven and bake an additional 20 to 25 minutes, or until the top is golden and the curd is firm.

8. Cool the lemon bars completely on a rack. Run a knife around the sides of the pan to prevent sticking. When cool, cut the lemon bars and remove them from the pan. Put confectioners' sugar in a strainer and sprinkle on top of the bars before serving.

Yield: Approximately 36 bars

VARIATIONS

Frosted Bars: *Blend 1 cup confectioners' sugar with 3 tablespoons lemon juice to form a light frosting. Spread frosting over the cooled bars instead of sprinkling with confectioners' sugar.*

Lemon-Coconut Bars: *Mix 1 cup shredded sweetened coconut into the lemon mixture (step 5).*

TIPS

For easier cleanup, line the pan with aluminum foil, leaving a one-inch overhang, before adding the dough. After cooling, lift the foil and the lemon bars out of the pan together.

One medium lemon yields almost one-quarter cup of juice and about one tablespoon of grated zest.

To get more juice from a lemon, microwave it on high for ten seconds or put it in a bowl of hot water for thirty minutes. Then roll it on the counter, pressing lightly, before squeezing the juice.

Always grate the lemon zest before squeezing the lemon for juice.

Grate only the yellow portion of the lemon peel. The white portion, known as the pith, is very bitter.

The crust can be easily made in a food processor fitted with a metal chopping blade. Pulse the sugar and flour five times. Add the butter and process until the dough just comes together (twenty to thirty seconds). Do not allow the dough to form a ball.

Oatmeal Raisin Cookies

1½ cups all-purpose flour
1 teaspoon baking soda
½ teaspoon salt
1 teaspoon ground
   cinnamon
½ teaspoon ground nut-
   meg (optional)
1 cup (2 sticks) butter,
   softened
1 cup brown sugar, firmly
   packed
½ cup granulated sugar
1 teaspoon vanilla extract
2 eggs
3 cups uncooked oatmeal
1½ cups raisins

Homemade oatmeal cookies, full of spices and raisins, have a special place in most people's hearts.

Prep Time: 5 to 10 minutes
Baking Time: 8 to 12 minutes
Equipment: baking sheets, measuring spoons, measuring cups, medium bowl, large bowl, sturdy spoon, cooling rack (electric mixer or food processor, optional)

1. Preheat the oven to 375 degrees F. Take out the baking sheets.
2. In a medium bowl, mix the flour, baking soda, salt, cinnamon, and nutmeg. Set aside.
3. In a large bowl, using a sturdy spoon or an electric mixer, cream the butter until fluffy and lightened in color.
4. Add both sugars and beat until well blended.
5. Add the vanilla and eggs. Beat until thoroughly combined.
6. Gradually add the dry ingredients and mix well.
7. Gradually add the oatmeal and raisins until combined.
8. If time allows, refrigerate the dough until firm to prevent excess spreading, about 30 minutes.
9. Drop the dough by rounded tablespoons, 2 inches apart, onto the ungreased baking sheets.
10. Bake 8 to 12 minutes, or until the cookies are golden and the edges are lightly browned.
11. Let the cookies stand for 1 minute before transferring them to a cooling rack.

Yield: Approximately 30 cookies (depending on size of cookies)

Gingery Good: *Add 2 tablespoons finely chopped crystallized ginger to the dry ingredients (step 2) for spicy ginger flavor.*

Nutty Oaties: *Add 1/2 cup chopped nuts (step 7) for added flavor and crunch.*

Chocolate Chip Oaties: *Substitute chocolate chips for the raisins.*

Colorful Oaties: *Use equal amounts of dark and golden raisins for colorful cookies.*

TIPS

These cookies can also be mixed in a food processor fitted with a metal chopping blade. Mix in the raisins by hand.

Use either quick-cooking or old-fashioned oats. Old-fashioned oats make chewier cookies; quick-cooking oats absorb moisture faster and tend to make crisper cookies. Do not use instant oatmeal.

If you refrigerate the dough before baking, wait to preheat the oven until fifteen minutes before you are ready to bake.

For giant cookies, use a one-quarter-cup measuring cup and drop the dough four inches apart. Add approximately three minutes to the baking time.

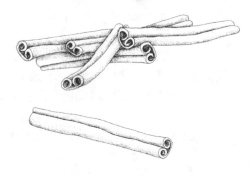

Chocolate–Chocolate Chip Cookies

2¼ cups all-purpose flour
1 teaspoon baking soda
½ teaspoon salt
¾ cup unsweetened cocoa
1 cup (2 sticks) butter, softened
¾ cup granulated sugar
¾ cup brown sugar, firmly packed
2 teaspoons vanilla extract
2 eggs
2 cups semisweet chocolate chips or chocolate chunks

Taking the chocolate chip cookie one step further can't be too far for real chocolate lovers.

Prep Time: 5 to 10 minutes
Baking Time: 7 to 12 minutes
Equipment: baking sheets, measuring spoons, measuring cups, medium bowl, large bowl, sturdy spoon, cooling rack (electric mixer or food processor, optional)

1. Preheat the oven to 350 degrees F. Take out the baking sheets.
2. In a medium bowl, mix the flour, baking soda, salt, and cocoa. Set aside.
3. In a large bowl, using a sturdy spoon or an electric mixer, cream the butter until fluffy and lightened in color.
4. Add both sugars and beat until well blended.
5. Add the vanilla and eggs. Beat until thoroughly combined.
6. Gradually add the dry ingredients and mix well.
7. Stir in the chocolate chips.
8. If time allows, refrigerate the dough until firm to prevent excess spreading, about 30 minutes.
9. Drop the dough by rounded tablespoons, 2 inches apart, onto the ungreased baking sheets.
10. Bake 7 to 12 minutes, or until the cookies are set, being careful not to burn them. The centers will feel slightly firm to the touch.
11. Let the cookies stand for 1 minute before transferring them to a cooling rack.

Yield: Approximately 48 cookies (depending on size of cookies)

The First Book of Baking

Black and Whites: *Substitute white chocolate chips for the semisweet chips.*

Peanut Butter Chippers: *Substitute peanut butter chips for the semisweet chips.*

After-Dinner Mint: *Substitute mint chocolate chips for semisweet chips.*

Ice Cream Sandwiches: *Spread softened ice cream between two large cookies for a wonderful summertime treat. Freeze until ready to use.*

TIPS

These cookies can also be mixed in a food processor fitted with a metal chopping blade.

If you refrigerate the dough before baking, wait to preheat the oven until fifteen minutes before you are ready to bake.

For giant cookies, use a one-quarter-cup measuring cup and drop the dough four inches apart. Add approximately three minutes to the baking time.

The chocolate color makes it more difficult to judge readiness. Be sure to start checking the cookies before the minimum cooking time, and watch for burning edges and bottoms. Use insulated baking sheets or double-stack two sheets to prevent burned bottoms.

Cookies will puff during baking and flatten while cooling.

Peanut Butter Cookies

⤫ ⤬

1 ½ cups all-purpose flour
1 teaspoon baking soda
½ teaspoon salt
½ cup (1 stick) butter, softened
½ cup brown sugar, firmly
 packed
½ cup granulated sugar
1 teaspoon vanilla extract
1 egg
1 cup peanut butter,
 creamy or chunky
 style

Loaded with peanut butter, these soft and chewy cookies are a taste sensation. What could be better than peanut butter in cookies? Well, maybe some chocolate chips added in . . .

Prep Time: 5 to 10 minutes
Baking Time: 8 to 12 minutes
Equipment: baking sheets, measuring spoons, measuring cups, medium bowl, large bowl, sturdy spoon, fork, cooling rack (electric mixer or food processor, optional)

1. Preheat the oven to 375 degrees F. Lightly grease the baking sheets.
2. In a medium bowl, mix the flour, baking soda, and salt. Set aside.
3. In a large bowl, using a sturdy spoon or an electric mixer, cream the butter until fluffy and lightened in color.
4. Add both sugars and beat until well blended.
5. Add the vanilla, egg, and peanut butter. Beat until thoroughly combined.
6. Gradually add the dry ingredients and mix well.
7. If time allows, refrigerate the dough until firm to prevent excess spreading, about 30 minutes.
8. Shape the dough into balls 1 ½ inches in diameter, and space them 2 inches apart on the baking sheets.

9. Flatten the cookies and gently press a crisscross pattern on top with a wet fork.
10. Bake 8 to 12 minutes, or until the cookies are golden and the edges are lightly browned.
11. Let the cookies stand for 1 minute before transferring them to a cooling rack.

Yield: Approximately 40 cookies (depending on size of cookies)

VARIATIONS

Chocolatey Good: *Add 1 cup of semisweet chocolate, milk chocolate, or white chocolate chips to the batter (step 6).*

Even Nuttier: *Add 1 cup chopped peanuts for added flavor and crunch (step 6), or try 1 cup peanut butter chips (step 6).*

TIPS

These cookies can also be mixed in a food processor fitted with a metal chopping blade.

If you refrigerate the dough before baking, wait to preheat the oven until fifteen minutes before you are ready to bake.

Drop the dough by rounded tablespoons for more irregularly shaped cookies.

For giant cookies, use a one-quarter-cup measuring cup and drop the dough four inches apart. Add approximately three minutes to the baking time.

Rice Crispy Marshmallow Bars

⚬⚬ ⚬⚬

3   tablespoons butter
10   ounces marshmallows,
         approximately 40
6   cups puffed rice cereal

With no baking required, these chewy treats are a snap, crackle, and pop to make.

Prep Time: 10 to 15 minutes
Equipment: 13 by 9 by 2-inch baking pan, measuring spoons, measuring cups, medium saucepan or microwave-safe bowl

1. Lightly grease a 13 by 9 by 2-inch baking pan.
2. In a medium saucepan, melt the butter over low heat.
3. Add the marshmallows, coat with butter, and stir until melted and smooth. Remove from the heat.
4. Add the rice cereal to the marshmallow mixture in three batches, stirring to coat well after each addition.
5. Using a lightly greased spatula, transfer the mixture to the baking pan.
6. Distribute the mixture evenly in the pan.
7. Cool completely in the pan before cutting.

Yield: Approximately 36 bars

For easier cleanup, line the pan with aluminum foil, leaving a one-inch overhang, before adding the cereal mixture. After cooling, lift the foil and the crispy bars out of the pan together and peel off the foil.

Rice Crispy bars can also be made in the microwave. In a microwave-safe bowl, melt the butter and marshmallows together on high for two minutes. Stir to combine, and microwave one minute more. Stir until smooth. Continue with step 4.

To spread the marshmallow mixture in the pan more easily, cover it with a piece of waxed paper and press lightly until the mixture is evenly distributed.

Use fresh marshmallows for best results.

Shortbread

❧ ❧

½ cup (1 stick) butter,
    softened
¼ cup confectioners' sugar
1 teaspoon vanilla extract
1 cup all-purpose flour
⅛ teaspoon salt

These buttery cookies of Scottish heritage are traditionally shaped in a large circle and cut into decorative wedges.

Prep Time: 10 to 15 minutes
Baking Time: 20 to 25 minutes
Equipment: baking sheet or 8- or 9-inch pie pan, measuring spoons, measuring cups, large bowl, sturdy spoon, knife, fork, cooling rack (electric mixer or food processor, optional)

1. Preheat the oven to 350 degrees F. Take out a baking sheet or pie pan.
2. In a large bowl, using a sturdy spoon or an electric mixer, cream the butter until fluffy and lightened in color.
3. Add the confectioners' sugar and vanilla, and beat until well blended.
4. Gradually add the flour and salt, and mix thoroughly.
5. Gently pat the dough into a 9-inch-diameter circle on an ungreased baking sheet, or fit the dough into a pie pan. Before baking, use a sharp knife to score the dough into 8 or 12 wedges (as if you are slicing a pie). Do not cut all the way through the dough. Using the tines of a fork, make a border around the outside edge of the circle and decoratively prick the cookies a few times to prevent puffing during baking.
6. Bake 20 to 25 minutes, or until the cookies and the edges are pale golden. Do not overbake; they should not brown.

7. Remove the shortbread from the oven and, while still warm, cut into wedges along the score marks with a sharp knife.
8. Let the shortbread stand for 2 minutes before transferring it to a cooling rack.

Yield: Approximately 8 to 12 cookies (depending on size of cookies)

VARIATIONS

Rolled Cookies: *After mixing, scrape the dough onto a lightly floured surface. Roll out the dough ¼ inch thick with a lightly floured rolling pin, turning often to prevent sticking. Use floured cookie cutters or a sharp knife to cut the dough into desired shapes. Carefully transfer the cookies to ungreased baking sheets and bake for 15 to 20 minutes, or until golden. Cool 1 minute and transfer to a rack.*

Drop Cookies: *Shape the dough into 1½-inch balls, place on an ungreased baking sheet, and flatten. Bake the cookies for 15 to 20 minutes, or until golden. Cool 1 minute and transfer to a rack.*

Lemon–Poppy Seed Shortbread: *Add 1 tablespoon poppy seeds and 1 teaspoon lemon zest to batter (step 4).*

Butter Pecan Shortbread: *Substitute brown sugar for confectioners' sugar and add 2 tablespoons finely chopped pecans (step 4).*

TIPS

These cookies can also be mixed in a food processor fitted with a metal chopping blade.

For slightly sweeter shortbread, use one-third cup confectioners' sugar.

If the cookie dough is too soft to work with, refrigerate or freeze it for five to ten minutes until it's less sticky.

Shortbread can also be made in round cake, springform, or tart pans. Springform and tart pans with detachable bottoms make removing the cookies easy. Baking shortbread in a fluted tart pan adds a decorative touch.

Sugar Christmas Cookies

Cookies

2½ cups all-purpose flour
¼ teaspoon salt
1 teaspoon baking powder
1 cup (2 sticks) butter, softened
1 cup granulated sugar
2 teaspoons vanilla extract
1 egg
Colored sugar, sprinkles, or candies (optional)

Frosting (optional)

3 cups confectioners' sugar
2 to 3 tablespoons milk, plus additional milk
Food coloring (optional)

These cut and decorated cookies make holidays more festive. Eat them straight from the oven, or let your imagination run wild with icings, colored sugars, and other decorations.

Prep Time: 15 to 20 minutes, plus an hour or more to chill
Baking Time: 8 to 13 minutes
Equipment: baking sheets, measuring spoons, measuring cups, medium bowl, large bowl, sturdy spoon, rolling pin, cookie cutters or sharp knife, cooling rack (electric mixer or food processor, pastry bag, small spatula or brush, optional)

1. In a medium bowl, mix the flour, salt, and baking powder. Set aside.
2. In a large bowl, using a sturdy spoon or an electric mixer, cream the butter until fluffy and lightened in color.
3. Add the sugar and beat until well blended.
4. Add the vanilla and egg. Beat until thoroughly combined.
5. Gradually add the dry ingredients and mix well.
6. Scrape the dough onto a sheet of plastic wrap. It will be soft and sticky. Press the dough together to form a flat disk between ¼ and ½ inch thick. Wrap tightly and refrigerate until firm, 1 to 2 hours.
7. When the cookies are ready to roll out, preheat the oven to 350 degrees F. Take out the baking sheets.
8. On a lightly floured surface, with a lightly floured rolling pin, roll out the dough ⅛ to ¼ inch thick, lifting and turning it frequently to prevent sticking (add additional flour if necessary to prevent sticking). With flour-dipped cookie cutters or a sharp knife, cut the dough into desired shapes. Carefully transfer the dough to ungreased baking sheets.

The First Book of Baking

9. Decorate the cookies with colored sugars, sprinkles, or candies. If decorating cookies with icing, bake the cookies before frosting.
10. Bake 8 to 13 minutes, or until the cookies are firm to the touch and the edges are golden.
11. Let the cookies stand for 1 minute before transferring them to a cooling rack. Cool completely before frosting.
12. Frost the cookies (optional). In a small bowl, combine the confectioners' sugar and milk. Mix until smooth and creamy, but stiff enough that the frosting does not flow from a spoon (if necessary, add additional milk or sugar, $1/2$ teaspoon at a time, to reach the desired consistency). Use a pastry bag with a small rounded tip (or fill a zip-top plastic bag with icing and cut off the bottom corner) to pipe decorations. To glaze cookies, add additional milk, $1/2$ teaspoon at a time, until the mixture flows from a spoon. For colored icing or glaze, divide the frosting into small bowls and add food coloring, a few drops at a time. Spread the icing or glaze with a small spatula or brush. If you are piping frosting on top of a glaze, wait for the glaze to dry first. Allow the decorated cookies to dry completely before storing (about 2 hours).

Yield: Approximately 48 cookies (depending on size of cookies)

VARIATION

Painted Cookies: *To paint color on cookies, mix 2 tablespoons evaporated milk with a few drops of food coloring (use separate little bowls for different colors). Paint the mixture on the cookies before baking.*

TIPS

To make colored sugar, just add small amounts of food coloring to granulated sugar.

These cookies can also be mixed in a food processor fitted with a metal chopping blade.

A ruler is handy for measuring the thickness of rolled-out dough.

If you don't have cookie cutters in the shapes you want, make patterns out of cardboard and cut around them.

If you want to hang cookies from the Christmas tree, make a small hole in the dough before baking.

To prevent the dough from being too sticky to roll out, refrigerate it until firm. If the dough seems excessively sticky after mixing, work in a little extra flour before chilling.

Chilled dough should be moist enough to roll easily. It should not crack when rolled. If the dough is too cold, let it sit at room temperature until firm but workable. If the dough becomes sticky during rolling, add flour to your rolling surface and rolling pin.

Cookies can be rolled out on a lightly floured surface or rolled between sheets of waxed paper or plastic wrap (lightly flour first, if necessary). Be careful not to overwork the dough, or the cookies will be tough. Roll out small portions of dough at a time, refrigerating the remainder so it remains firm. Don't reroll scraps more than once or twice, or the cookies will be tough (chill first if necessary).

Do not roll the dough too thin—one-quarter-inch-thick dough is easy to work with and resists tears.

Beginning cookie makers should avoid cookie cutters with intricate designs. The dough will be more difficult to transfer from the cutter to the baking sheets.

If the sugar has trouble adhering before baking, lightly coat the cookies with beaten egg whites first. This will also give the cookies a shinier crust.

Set up a design center with cookie cutters, colored sprinkles, candies, frosting, and other decorations. Line the work surface with waxed paper or foil for easier cleanup.

Combine decorating techniques. Glaze cookies, and then pipe with different colored icing or sprinkle with colored sugar or candies.

For an easy design, drizzle glaze to create interesting zigzag patterns.

Cookies do not have to be rolled out. You can also form them into one-and-one-half-inch balls, roll them in sugar, flatten to one-quarter inch thick, and bake.

CAKES

❧ ❧

No matter what the occasion, it's just not a party without a cake. A cake makes any event a celebration. The dilemma should never be whether or not to make a cake, it should be which cake to make! With airy angel food cakes, creamy cheesecakes, buttery layer cakes, and crumbly spice-filled coffee cakes to choose from, it's difficult to pick just one.

Baking the cake of your choice has never been easier. Here you'll find instructions for perfectly beaten egg whites to make sponge cakes spongier than ever as well as heaps of helpful hints for frosting and decorating layer cakes.

Equipment

PANS

- Use medium-weight metal cake pans.
- Pans with shiny finishes reflect heat away from the cake and produce tender, lighter crusts. Pans with nonstick finishes make removing cakes easier.
- The recipes in this book call for straight-sided, 1½-inch deep, 9-inch layer pans; a 9-inch spring-form pan; a 10-inch tube pan; a 10-inch Bundt pan; and a 9 by 5 by 3-inch loaf pan.

- Always use the correct size pan. To check the size, measure the pan across the top inside diameter with a ruler.

- An electric mixer does an excellent job of creaming butter and sugar together and aerating the batter. The air incorporated into the batter gives the cake its light and fine-grained texture. Handheld mixers are usually less powerful than standing mixers and might take longer to achieve the desired effect.
- A layer of parchment paper placed in the pan prevents cakes from sticking and keeps cake bottoms from overbrowning. For a perfect fit when lining cake pans with parchment, trace the base of the pan on the paper before cutting.
- Magi-Cake Strips are a fabulous baking aid. These cloth strips, made with aluminized fabric, are moistened and placed around the outside of the baking pan. The moisture and insulation from the strips slows down the heat transfer of the metal sides against the batter and produces more evenly cooked cakes. Strips are especially useful with dark pans, which can cause cakes to have a thick, dark crust.
- Cooling racks allow air to circulate freely on all sides of the cake for proper cooling.

Ingredients

FLOUR

- Depending on the recipe, use either bleached or unbleached all-purpose flour or cake flour. Cake flour is finely milled soft-wheat flour, which contains less protein and more starch than all-purpose flour. It is used for cakes that have a lighter and more delicate texture.

The First Book of Baking

- Cake flour has a tendency to lump together, so it is necessary to sift or strain it before using.
- To substitute all-purpose flour for cake flour, use one cup less two tablespoons of all-purpose flour for every cup of cake flour called for in the recipe. To replace all-purpose flour with cake flour, add two tablespoons of cake flour for every cup of all-purpose flour called for.

OTHER INGREDIENTS

- For optimal results, use ingredients at room temperature unless noted.
- Leave most refrigerated items out for one to two hours to achieve the proper temperature.
- Use unsalted butter for a more authentic bakery flavor. Butter softened to room temperature (approximately 70 degrees F) will be malleable but should not lose its shape or become oily. To soften butter quickly, cut the butter into pieces or microwave it for fifteen to twenty seconds.
- Use USDA large eggs. To quickly bring eggs to room temperature, place them in very warm water for five to ten minutes.
- Use pure, not imitation, extracts.
- Use unsweetened cocoa powder. To prevent lumps, always stir the cocoa before adding it to a batter.
- Baker's Joy, a nonstick spray that contains flour, is designed to grease and flour pans quickly. It is available in many supermarkets.

Let Them Eat Cake

GETTING READY

- Prepare the oven. If you are using one pan, position the oven rack in the middle of the oven. If you are baking two pans at a time, use the middle rack if it allows at least one to two inches between the pans and between the oven walls. If there is not enough room on one shelf, position two racks near the center of the oven, making sure to leave enough room between shelves for the cakes to rise.

- Always preheat the oven for at least fifteen minutes before baking.
- Prepare the baking pan. Many cakes need to be baked immediately after mixing, so the pan needs to be ready to go.
- Greasing the cake pan with nonstick vegetable spray, softened butter, or shortening prevents cakes from sticking. When greasing a tube or Bundt pan, make sure to get into the corners.
- Flouring the pan (when called for) gives the batter something to grip to help it rise. To flour a pan, sprinkle one to two tablespoons of flour in the pan after greasing. Swirl or shake the pan until all surfaces are coated. Remove the excess flour by tapping the pan, upside down, over the sink.
- When baking a chocolate cake, use unsweetened cocoa powder for coating the pan instead of flour. This gives cakes a little chocolate boost and is a better color match.

Mixing the Batter

- One minute of beating time with a mixer equals 150 strokes by hand.
- Creaming the butter with sugar forms a smooth mixture that will combine easily with the other ingredients, and beats in air to help the cake rise. Butter and sugar should be beaten together for one to two minutes at medium speed, until fluffy and smooth. The butter's color will lighten and look almost white. The friction of the sugar beating against the butter will create little air pockets that give the cake its light and airy texture.

- Add dry ingredients alternately with liquid (one-third of the dry ingredients and half of the liquid at a time), beating well after each addition for adequate blending. The sequential additions of flour helps the butter absorb the liquid better. Begin and end mixing with the dry ingredients.
- Although thorough beating is important when creaming butter, sugar, and eggs, mix the dry ingredients just until combined with the batter. Overmixing dry ingredients will undo much of the aeration achieved through creaming.
- For better control and to prevent overmixing, you may choose to cream the butter and sugar with a mixer and complete the recipe manually, gently folding in the dry ingredients with a spatula or with open and extended fingers.
- For a uniform cake batter, it is very important to scrape down the sides and bottom of the bowl periodically, whether using an electric mixer or beating by hand.

BEATING AND FOLDING EGG WHITES

- Beaten egg whites, when properly whipped and gently folded into the batter, give cakes added volume and a light, spongy texture. The following guidelines will help you understand the beating and folding process.
- Cold eggs are easier to separate, but eggs beat to greater volume when they are at room temperature (about 70 degrees F). So separate the eggs at the beginning of the recipe, and let them sit to lose their chill as you work.
- When separating eggs, have four bowls lined up: one for whites, one for yolks, one in case the yolk breaks during separation, and one larger bowl to collect all the egg whites after they have been successfully separated.
- To separate eggs easily, carefully crack the shell in two. Using the shells as cups, pour the yolk from shell to shell, letting the white drip into a bowl. Alternatively, open the

egg into the palm of your hand, separate your fingers slightly, and let the white run through your fingers into a bowl, leaving the yolk in your hand.

- If any yolk gets into the egg white, use an empty shell to remove it.
- For egg whites to reach their maximum volume, there must be no trace of egg yolk in the whites, and the bowl and utensils must be clean, dry, and totally free of grease or fat.
- To bring egg whites to room temperature quickly, set the bowl of whites in a large bowl of very warm water and gently stir for a few minutes.
- Beat egg whites only when you're ready to use them; if they stand, they will become watery and deflate.
- Beaten egg whites should more than triple in volume. Whip them in a bowl that is large enough to accommodate the added volume.
- If possible, beat egg whites in a copper bowl. A chemical reaction occurs between copper and egg-white albumen that stabilizes the foam. If you don't have a copper bowl, use stainless steel. Do not use glass, ceramic, or plastic bowls, all of which have a tendency to hold grease.
- Adding cream of tartar and sugar during beating also stabilizes the egg whites and allows them to attain greater volume with less chance of overbeating.
- When adding sugar to egg whites, add it gradually, approximately one or two tablespoons every ten to twenty seconds, until it is incorporated. When all the sugar has been added, beat just until stiff peaks form when you stop and lift the beaters. Rub the egg whites between your fingers to make sure they are smooth and that the sugar has been fully absorbed.
- Properly beaten egg whites look like whipped marshmallow topping or fluffy shaving cream. Beaten egg whites will be firm enough to support the weight of a whole egg in its shell and should stay in place if the bowl is turned on its side.

- It is better to slightly underbeat egg whites than to risk over-beating them. Overbeaten egg whites will look dry and cottony, and will partially return to liquid form. To remedy overbeating, add another egg white and beat until the proper consistency is achieved. If this doesn't happen within one minute, beat in another white.
- To prevent overbeating, finish beating by hand, using a wire whisk, once the egg whites form soft peaks.
- It is best to fold in beaten egg whites in two or more additions.
- To fold in egg whites, use a large rubber spatula or your hand. Begin in the middle of the bowl and move the spatula, or your hand with open and extended fingers, down toward the bottom of the bowl then up the side and out over the top. Turn the blade and your wrist so they are upside down when they come out of the bowl. This brings the bottom batter up and over the ingredients to be folded in. Rotate the bowl slightly and repeat until both mixtures are just combined and there are no masses of egg whites, flour, or batter (about four rotations).
- Use caution when folding in the egg whites. The whites are beaten to add volume and to lighten the batter. Take care not to deflate them.
- If you're folding egg whites into a very thick mixture, it is helpful to blend a small amount of egg whites into the mixture before folding, to lighten the batter and make folding easier.
- Bake cakes with beaten egg whites right away or they will lose their volume.
- Freeze extra egg whites in ice cube trays, and store in air-tight plastic bags until they are needed.

FILLING THE PAN

- Fill layer, springform, and sheet cake pans between one-half and two-thirds full. Fill Bundt and tube pans two-thirds full.

With too little batter, the cake won't rise or brown properly. With too much batter, the pan can overflow and the edges will overcook before the center is done. Use any excess batter for cupcakes.

- When the pan is filled with batter, smooth the top with a spatula and run the batter up the sides a little. Leave the batter slightly lower in the center for a more even finished product.
- Before putting the batter in the oven, lift the cake pan a few inches above the counter and gently drop it to dislodge air bubbles, which can expand into holes during baking. Don't do this with cakes that use beaten egg whites—you need the air for leavening.

BAKING

- Place pans in the oven, leaving at least one to two inches between the pans and between the walls of the oven for better heat circulation. If you're baking on two shelves, stagger the pans so the heat can circulate between them, but keep them toward the center of the oven.
- Don't try to save time by increasing the oven temperature for faster results. You'll end up with an overcooked outside and an undercooked inside.
- If you're baking on two shelves, or if your oven heats unevenly, rotate the cakes midway through baking. Make sure to open and shut the oven door as quickly as possible.
- Try not to look in the oven until five to ten minutes before the minimum baking time (unless you smell the cake burning). Opening and shutting the oven doors while baking affects the oven temperature, letting cooler air in and hot air out, and could cause the cake to fall. Excessive opening will also add time to the baking period.
- If a cake has a long cooking time, cover the pan with lightly greased foil after forty minutes to prevent overbrowning.

Testing Doneness

- A cake is done when the top looks dry, a toothpick inserted into the center comes out with no crumbs clinging, and the cake springs back (leaving no depression) when lightly touched in the center.
- If the cake has started shrinking from the sides of its pan, it is done. If the other signs are present, do not wait for this to happen or the cake could be slightly dry.
- If a toothpick comes out with thick, damp batter clinging to it, the cake will need about ten more minutes of baking. If the toothpick has sticky crumbs on it, three to five more minutes should be enough.
- If a toothpick is too short for testing a cake in a deep pan, use a wooden skewer or a clean broom straw.

Cooling and Removing the Cake from the Pan

- Unless noted, place the cake on a cooling rack for fifteen minutes before taking it out of the pan.
- To remove a cake from its pan, run a sharp knife or frosting spatula around the sides of the pan to prevent sticking. Then cover the pan with an inverted cooling rack (or your hand) and flip it over. The cake should drop out. To reinvert the cake, so it is right side up, cover again with a cooling rack (or your hand) and repeat the process. Let the cake finish cooling on the rack.
- If it is difficult to get a baked cake out of the pan, place the warm pan on a hot, wet towel for added steam.

Frosting a Two-Layer Cake

- Cake frosting should be soft, pliant, and smooth enough to spread without tearing the cake.
- To color the frosting, add food coloring or paste color a little at a time. Stir briskly to evenly distribute the color.

- Cakes must be completely cooled before frosting.
- Freezing a cake for an hour before frosting it makes it more stable and reduces crumbs.
- Before frosting a cake, position one layer upside down on a cake plate or a stiff piece of cardboard slightly larger than the cake, so the top is totally flat. If possible, put the cake plate on a revolving cake-decorating turntable or lazy Susan for easier access. Rotating spice carousels also work well.
- To avoid a messy cake plate, slip four or more three-inch-wide strips of waxed paper or aluminum foil under the cake's edges before frosting.
- Always brush loose crumbs from the cake with a pastry brush before frosting.
- Using a frosting spatula, an offset spatula, or a dinner knife, spread the frosting about one-quarter-inch thick on top of bottom layer. Use light back and forth strokes with your spatula. Try not to lift the spatula—it could pull the crust away from the cake.
- As a general rule, allow three-quarters to one cup of frosting or filling between layers.
- If the filling between layers is a different flavor or color than the rest of the frosting, leave a one-inch border around the cake's edge. Place a small amount of frosting around the edge of the filling to prevent it from spilling out.
- After you have applied the filling, place the second cake layer, rounded side up, on top of the filling. If the top layer is very uneven, carefully cut a thin horizontal slice off the top and place it bottom side up. Again, brush loose crumbs with a pastry brush.
- If the cake has an excessive amount of loose crumbs, coat it with a thin layer of diluted frosting to act as a sealer. Wait for it to dry completely before continuing to frost.

The First Book of Baking

- Spread frosting, no more than one-quarter inch thick, over the sides of the cake, smoothing it with the edge of the knife or frosting spatula.
- It's easier to smooth the frosting if you move the cake rather than the spatula. If you're using a revolving platform, turn the cake with one hand and smooth the frosting with a spatula that is held still in the other.
- Put the remaining frosting on the top of the cake. Decoratively texture the frosting or make a smooth finish. If necessary, trim off excess frosting around the circumference of the cake's top with the knife or spatula. Allow one-and-one-half to two cups of frosting for the top and sides.
- To even out the frosting and create a simple pattern, dab the frosted cake, a small area at a time, with damp textured paper towels (use three layers of towels to prevent tears). For a totally smooth finish, use a wet spatula to level frosting.
- If the frosting becomes too thick to spread easily, add a few drops of liquid.
- When the cake is decorated, gently pull out waxed paper or foil. Wipe off any frosting smudges on the plate.
- A homemade cake is a treat—don't worry if the frosting isn't picture perfect.

ADDITIONAL DECORATIONS

- To decorate the sides of the cake and hide any frosting errors, use any of the following: colored sugar, sprinkles, mini chocolate chips, grated chocolate, cookie crumbs, chopped nuts, or shredded coconut. Cup the decorations in your palm and press them into the frosting until they are firmly embedded but not buried.
- Decorate the top of a cake with fresh fruit (plain or dipped in chocolate); marzipan fruit; edible, unsprayed fresh or sugared flowers; large candies; store-bought edible decorations; animal

crackers; or whole nuts (plain or dipped in chocolate). Or use any of the garnishes recommended for side decoration.

- You can pipe extra frosting or whipped cream onto the cake with a pastry bag. Follow the manufacturer's directions or the instructions in a cake-decorating manual for the desired effect.
- To create a simple design, place a doily or stencil on top of the cake then dust with confectioners' sugar or cocoa.
- Use an interesting cake plate to show off your cake. Decorate the plate with fresh flowers or other embellishments.

SLICING

- Freezing a cake for an hour will make it firmer and easier to split.
- To split a cake evenly into two parts for a multilayered cake, use a serrated knife and a sawing motion. To prevent a lop-sided cut, mark the midpoint and insert a row of toothpicks around the cake to guide you. Alternately, circle the cake with waxed dental floss where you want to cut it, cross the ends, and pull gently but firmly. The floss will cut through the cake.
- Slice frosted layer cakes with a long, thin, sharp knife. For easiest slicing, dip the knife in hot water and wipe it dry before cutting. If water is not available, wipe the knife well between slices.
- Use a serrated knife to cut pound, Bundt, sponge, and angel food cakes.

STORING

- Most unfrosted cakes, if tightly wrapped, will stay fresh at room temperature for several days. They also freeze well. The exceptions are coffee cakes, which will become stale if not eaten or frozen soon after baking; and cheesecakes, which should be stored in the refrigerator.

- Use an inexpensive clear plastic shower cap, like the ones you get in hotels, to wrap around leftover cake. The elasticized edges fit neatly and securely around the cake plate.
- Protect frosted cakes by putting toothpicks on the top and around the sides of the cake before wrapping. An airtight cake dome also works well.
- After a cake has been cut, place a piece of plastic wrap or waxed paper directly against the cut side to keep the unserved portion fresh.
- Cakes with perishable fillings or frostings, like cream cheese or whipped cream, must be refrigerated.
- To protect frosting when freezing a decorated cake, let the cake chill uncovered in the freezer until the frosting is firm. Wrap it tightly and return to the freezer.
- Before freezing, wrap cakes well in heavy-duty foil or freezer plastic wrap to protect them from air, moisture, and odors.
- Thaw frosted cakes unwrapped in the refrigerator or at room temperature to prevent condensation.
- Defrost unfrosted cakes in their wrapping.

Boston Cream Pie

Custard Filling

2	egg yolks
1/2	cup granulated sugar
2	tablespoons cornstarch
1	cup milk
1/8	teaspoon salt
1	tablespoon butter
1	tablespoon vanilla extract

Cake

1	cup all-purpose flour
1	teaspoon baking powder
1/4	teaspoon salt
3	tablespoons butter
1/2	cup milk
2	eggs
1	cup granulated sugar
1	teaspoon vanilla extract

Chocolate Glaze

1/2	cup semisweet or bitter-sweet chocolate, chopped
3	tablespoons butter
2	tablespoons light corn syrup

This dessert sandwiches creamy custard between layers of spongy vanilla cake, and tops it all off with a shiny chocolate glaze. Many people have wondered why it is called a pie, but this cake is so good no one really cares what it's called!

Prep Time: 20 to 25 minutes, plus 2 to 4 hours to chill
Baking Time: 15 to 20 minutes
Equipment: two 9-inch cake pans, measuring spoons, measuring cups, heavy-bottomed medium-sized saucepan, 2 medium bowls, large bowl, electric mixer, spatula, cooling rack, knife

1. Prepare the custard. In a medium saucepan, beat the egg yolks. Add the sugar and cornstarch and mix well. Stir in the milk, salt, and butter.

2. Place the saucepan over medium heat and cook 5 to 7 minutes, stirring constantly, until the mixture is bubbling and thick.

3. Remove the pan from the heat and stir in the vanilla. Transfer the mixture to a medium bowl. Place a piece of plastic wrap directly on the surface of the custard to prevent a film from forming, and refrigerate for 2 to 4 hours.

4. Prepare the cake. Preheat the oven to 350 degrees F. Lightly grease the bottoms of two 9-inch cake pans.

5. In a medium bowl, mix the flour, baking powder, and salt. Set aside.

6. In a saucepan, heat the butter and milk until just boiling. Set aside.

7. In a large bowl, beat the eggs with an electric mixer on medium speed for 1 minute.

8. Add the sugar gradually and beat until thick and pale. Add the vanilla.

9. On low speed, slowly pour the hot milk into the egg mixture. Mix until blended.

10. Add the dry ingredients gradually.

11. When everything has been added, scrape the bowl and beaters with a spatula and mix until blended and smooth (about 5 seconds). Do not overmix. The batter will be very thin.

12. Divide the batter evenly between the prepared pans and place them on the middle rack of the oven, leaving 2 inches between the pans and the oven walls. The batter will fill the pan less than halfway.

13. Bake for 15 to 20 minutes, or until the cakes are lightly golden, a toothpick inserted in the center comes out clean, and the cakes spring back when lightly touched. Do not wait for the cakes to pull away from the sides.

14. Cool the cakes in their pans on a rack for 15 minutes. Loosen the sides with a thin knife and carefully remove the cake layers. Cool completely on a rack before assembling.

15. Prepare the chocolate glaze. In a saucepan, combine the chocolate, butter, and corn syrup over low heat, stirring until smooth. Remove from the heat and cool until thickened, 10 to 15 minutes.

16. Assemble the cake. Place one cake layer, right side up, on a serving plate. Top with the custard filling. Place the second layer, right side up, on top of the custard and pour the chocolate on top, allowing the glaze to drip down the sides, if desired. Let the glaze set for 10 minutes. Refrigerate if not serving immediately.

Yield: Serves 12 to 14

(Continues)

VARIATION

Banana Boston Cream Pie: *Place 2 medium bananas, cut into ¹/₄-inch slices, on top of the filling.*

TIPS

If cornstarch isn't in your cupboard, substitute four tablespoons of flour.

Line the cake pans with lightly greased parchment or waxed paper to prevent sticking.

For a smaller cake, use eight-inch cake pans. Add three to five minutes to the baking time.

If you have refrigerated the cake, let it stand at room temperature fifteen to thirty minutes before serving.

Use Magi-Cake Strips around the sides of the pan to prevent the outside crust from overbaking.

German Chocolate Cake

Cake

4 ounces German's Sweet Chocolate (1 package)
½ cup water
2½ cups all-purpose flour
1 teaspoon baking soda
½ teaspoon salt
1 cup (2 sticks) butter, softened
2 cups granulated sugar
1 teaspoon vanilla extract
4 egg yolks, room temperature
1 cup buttermilk
4 egg whites, room temperature

Frosting

1 cup (8 ounces) evaporated milk
1 cup granulated sugar
½ cup (1 stick) butter
3 egg yolks, lightly beaten
1 teaspoon vanilla extract
1 cup pecans, finely chopped
1½ cups shredded sweetened coconut

Although many people think this triple-decker cake is named for its country of origin, it is actually named for Mr. German, the inventor of a type of sweet chocolate. This cake's trademark is its delicious coconut-pecan frosting.

Prep Time: 20 to 30 minutes
Baking Time: 25 to 35 minutes
Equipment: three 9-inch cake pans, measuring spoons, measuring cups, medium bowl, 2 large bowls, electric mixer, spatula, cooling rack, knife, medium saucepan

1. Preheat the oven to 350 degrees F. Lightly grease and flour three 9-inch cake pans.
2. Prepare the cake. Melt the chocolate in the water until smooth. Set aside to cool.
3. In a medium bowl, mix the flour, baking soda, and salt. Set aside.
4. In a large bowl, cream the butter, sugar, and vanilla with an electric mixer on medium speed until light and fluffy, about 2 minutes, stopping twice to scrape the bowl and beaters.
5. Add the egg yolks one at a time, beating well after each addition.
6. Stir in the chocolate mixture until blended.
7. On low speed, alternate adding one-third of the dry ingredients with half of the buttermilk, mixing for 5 to 10 seconds after each addition. Do not blend each addition in fully before adding the next. When everything has been added, scrape the bowl and beaters and mix until blended and smooth (about 5 seconds). Do not overmix. Set aside.

(Continues)

8. In a large bowl, beat the egg whites with an electric mixer on high speed until stiff peaks form. Gently stir one-quarter of the whites into the batter. Using a spatula, or your open and extended fingers, fold in the remainder. The mixture will be a pale brown.

9. Divide the batter evenly between the prepared pans and smooth the tops with a spatula. Place the pans on the two center racks of the oven, leaving 2 inches between the pans and the oven walls.

10. Bake for 25 to 35 minutes, or until a toothpick inserted in the center comes out clean and the cakes spring back when lightly touched. Do not wait for the cakes to pull away from the sides.

11. Cool the cakes in their pans on a rack for 15 minutes. Loosen the sides with a thin knife and carefully remove the cake layers. Cool completely on a rack before frosting.

12. Prepare the frosting. In a medium saucepan, combine the evaporated milk, sugar, butter, egg yolks, and vanilla. Cook on medium heat, stirring constantly until thickened, bubbly, and golden brown, about 10 minutes. Remove from heat.

13. Stir in the pecans and coconut. Beat until cool.

14. Spread the frosting between layers and on top of the cake. This cake is not usually frosted on its sides.

Yield: Serves 12 to 14

VARIATION

Coconut-Almond Frosting: *Substitute chopped almonds for pecans.*

TIPS

Read "Beating and Folding Egg Whites," page 103, before starting the recipe.

The beaten egg whites give this cake a much lighter color and a spongier texture than most chocolate cakes.

The added steps of beating the egg whites and melting the chocolate make this cake's preparation more complicated and time-consuming than the basic chocolate layer cake (see recipe on page 124). Since the frosting is this cake's signature, you can successfully substitute the basic chocolate cake. Alternatively, use whole eggs instead of separated eggs (add when the yolks are called for). The cake will have a slightly different texture but will still be delicious.

Line the cake pans with lightly greased and floured parchment or waxed paper to prevent sticking.

Chocolate and water can be heated in the microwave or on the stove. If using a microwave, heat the mixture on high for one to two minutes, stirring every thirty seconds. Stir until the chocolate is completely melted. If using a stove, place the mixture over very low heat. Stir constantly until the chocolate has melted and the mixture is smooth.

Use Magi-Cake Strips around the sides of the pan to prevent the outside crust from overbaking.

Lemon–Poppy Seed Cake

Cake

3	cups all-purpose flour
1	teaspoon baking powder
1	teaspoon baking soda
½	teaspoon salt
1	cup (2 sticks) butter, softened
2	cups granulated sugar
5	eggs
2	tablespoons lemon zest, grated
2	tablespoons fresh lemon juice
1	cup sour cream
¼	cup poppy seeds

Glaze

½	cup fresh lemon juice, strained
½	cup granulated sugar

A refreshing dessert for lemon lovers. The poppy seeds add a hint of flavor and a surprising crunch.

Prep Time: 10 to 15 minutes
Baking Time: 65 to 75 minutes
Equipment: 10-inch Bundt or tube pan, measuring spoons, measuring cups, grater, medium bowl, large bowl, electric mixer, spatula, small bowl, cooling rack (pastry brush, optional)

1. Preheat the oven to 325 degrees F. Lightly grease a 10-inch Bundt pan.
2. Prepare the cake. In a medium bowl, mix the flour, baking powder, baking soda, and salt. Set aside.
3. In a large bowl, cream the butter and sugar with an electric mixer on medium speed until light and fluffy, about 2 minutes, stopping twice to scrape the bowl and beaters with a spatula.
4. Add the eggs one at a time, beating well after each addition.
5. Add the lemon zest and juice. Beat until the mixture is thick and pale yellow.
6. On low speed, alternate adding one-third of the dry ingredients with half of the sour cream, mixing for 5 to 10 seconds after each addition. Do not blend each addition in fully before adding the next. When everything has been added, scrape the bowl and beaters.
7. Add the poppy seeds and mix until blended and smooth (about 5 seconds). Do not overmix.
8. Pour the batter into the prepared pan and smooth the top with a spatula.

9. Bake for 65 to 75 minutes, or until the cake is lightly golden, a toothpick inserted in the center comes out clean, and the cake springs back when lightly touched. Loosely cover the cake with foil after 40 minutes to prevent it from overbrowning.
10. Cool the cake in its pan on a rack for 15 minutes.
11. Meanwhile, prepare the glaze. In a small bowl, stir the lemon juice and sugar until the sugar dissolves.
12. Remove the cake from the pan. Stir the glaze again and slowly drizzle it (or brush with a pastry brush) over the cake.

Yield: Serves 10 to 12

VARIATION

Creamy Lemon Glaze: *Melt 2 tablespoons butter and remove from heat. Sift or strain 1 cup of confectioners' sugar and combine with the melted butter. Stir until smooth. Add 2 to 3 tablespoons of lemon juice and stir until creamy. Pour the warm glaze over the cake.*

TIPS

One medium lemon yields almost one-quarter cup of juice and about one tablespoon grated zest.

Always grate the lemon zest before squeezing the lemon for juice.

Grate only the yellow portion of the lemon peel. The white portion, known as the pith, is very bitter.

To get more juice from a lemon, microwave it on high for ten seconds or put it in a bowl of hot water for thirty minutes. Then roll it on the counter, pressing lightly, before squeezing the juice. This breaks up the membrane inside the lemon so that the juices will release more easily when squeezed.

Soaking poppy seeds in the sour cream for an hour or more brings out their flavor.

Carrot Cake with Cream Cheese Frosting

Cake

2½ cups all-purpose flour
2 teaspoons baking powder
2 teaspoons baking soda
¼ teaspoon salt
2 teaspoons ground cinnamon
1½ cups (3 sticks) butter, softened
1 cup granulated sugar
1 cup brown sugar, firmly packed
1 tablespoon vanilla extract
3 eggs
3 cups carrots, grated (3 to 4 medium carrots)
¾ cup pineapple, crushed and drained
1 cup raisins
1 cup walnuts, chopped

Cream Cheese Frosting

15 ounces cream cheese, softened
½ cup (1 stick) butter, softened
1 teaspoon vanilla extract
3 cups confectioners' sugar

The combination of carrots, cinnamon, nuts, raisins, and pineapple creates the exceptional flavor, texture, and aroma of this cake. Cream cheese frosting provides the perfect complement. Move over, Bugs—carrots aren't just for bunnies anymore.

Prep Time: 15 to 20 minutes
Baking Time: 35 to 40 minutes
Equipment: two 9-inch cake pans, measuring spoons, measuring cups, grater or food processor, medium bowl, large bowl, electric mixer, spatula, cooling rack, knife

1. Preheat the oven to 350 degrees F. Lightly grease and flour two 9-inch cake pans.
2. Prepare the cake. In a medium bowl, mix the flour, baking powder, baking soda, salt, and cinnamon. Set aside.
3. In a large bowl, cream the butter, both sugars, and vanilla with an electric mixer on medium speed until light and fluffy, about 2 minutes, stopping twice to scrape the bowl and beaters with a spatula.
4. Add the eggs one at a time, beating well after each addition.
5. On low speed, add the dry ingredients gradually.
6. Add the carrots, pineapple, raisins, and walnuts. When everything has been added, scrape the bowl and beaters and mix until blended and smooth (about 5 seconds). Do not overmix.
7. Divide the batter evenly between the prepared pans and smooth the tops with a spatula. The batter will be thick. Place the pans on the middle rack of the oven, leaving 2 inches between the pans and the oven walls.

8. Bake for 35 to 40 minutes, or until a toothpick inserted in the center comes out clean and the cakes spring back when lightly touched. Do not wait for the cakes to pull away from the sides.

9. Cool the cakes in their pans on a rack for 15 minutes. Loosen the sides with a thin knife and carefully remove the cake layers. Cool completely on a rack before frosting.

10. Meanwhile, prepare the frosting. In a large bowl, beat the cream cheese, butter, and vanilla with an electric mixer on medium speed until well blended, stopping twice to scrape the bowl and beaters with a spatula.

11. On low speed, add the sugar gradually. Beat until fully incorporated and smooth. Frost the cake.

Yield: Serves 12 to 14

VARIATIONS

Crazy for Coconut: *Add 1 cup of shredded sweetened coconut with the carrots.*

Spice It Up: *To make a spice cake, omit the carrots, pineapple, raisins, and nuts, and add $1/2$ teaspoon each ginger, nutmeg, and cloves.*

That Lemon Zing: *Add 1 tablespoon fresh lemon juice (about $1/2$ lemon) to the frosting for a tangy taste.*

TIPS

Make sure to grate the carrots and chop the walnuts before you start mixing.

Line the cake pans with lightly greased and floured parchment or waxed paper to prevent sticking.

Use both dark and golden raisins for a more colorful presentation.

Lightly coat the raisins with flour for better suspension.

Hide frosting errors by placing finely chopped walnuts around the edges or sides of the cake.

Simply wash and grate the carrots—there's no need to peel them.

Use Magi-Cake Strips around the sides of the pan to prevent the outside crust from overbaking.

Yellow Layer Cake

This moist and buttery cake is not only perfect for birthdays, but will make any day you serve it a celebration!

2½ cups cake flour
2 teaspoons baking powder
½ teaspoon salt
¾ cup (1½ sticks) butter, softened
1½ cups granulated sugar
1 teaspoon vanilla extract
3 eggs
1 cup milk

Prep Time: 10 to 15 minutes
Baking Time: 25 to 35 minutes
Equipment: two 9-inch cake pans, measuring spoons, measuring cups, medium bowl, large bowl, electric mixer, spatula, cooling rack, knife

1. Preheat the oven to 350 degrees F. Lightly grease and flour two 9-inch cake pans.
2. In a medium bowl, mix the cake flour, baking powder, and salt. Set aside.
3. In a large bowl, cream the butter, sugar, and vanilla with an electric mixer on medium speed until light and fluffy, about 2 minutes, stopping twice to scrape the bowl and beaters with a spatula.
4. Add the eggs one at a time, beating well after each addition.
5. On low speed, alternate adding one-third of the dry ingredients with half of the milk, mixing for 5 to 10 seconds after each addition. Do not blend each addition in fully before adding the next. When everything has been added, scrape the bowl and beaters, and mix until blended and smooth (about 5 seconds). Do not overmix.
6. Divide the batter evenly between the prepared pans and smooth the tops with a spatula. Place the pans on the middle rack of the oven, leaving 2 inches between the pans and the oven walls.

7. Bake for 25 to 35 minutes, or until the cakes are lightly golden, a toothpick inserted in the center comes out clean, and the cakes spring back when lightly touched. Do not wait for the cakes to pull away from the sides.
8. Cool the cakes in their pans on a rack for 15 minutes. Loosen the sides with a thin knife and carefully remove the cake layers. Cool completely on a rack before frosting.

Yield: Serves 12 to 14

VARIATIONS

Chocolate Chip Cake: *Add 1 cup chocolate chips to the batter (after step 5).*

Coconut Cake: *Substitute coconut extract for vanilla and add 1 cup shredded sweetened coconut (after step 5).*

Cupcakes: *Line the muffin tins with paper or foil liners (liners keep cupcakes moist and make them easy to remove). Fill one-half to two-thirds full. Bake at 350 degrees F for 18 to 23 minutes, or until the tops are firm and a toothpick inserted into the center of a cupcake comes out clean. Cool the cupcakes completely in the tin on a rack. Remove and frost. Makes 24 cupcakes.*

Frosting and Filling: *Be creative with your frostings and fillings. This cake is great with chocolate or vanilla frosting and a fruit filling between layers.*

TIPS

If you're using a 13 by 9 by 2-inch pan, bake for thirty-five to forty-five minutes.

Line the cake pans with lightly greased and floured parchment or waxed paper to prevent sticking.

Use Magi-Cake Strips around the sides of the pan to prevent the outside crust from overbaking.

Chocolate Layer Cake

2 cups all-purpose flour
1 teaspoon baking soda
½ teaspoon salt
¾ cup unsweetened cocoa
½ cup (1 stick) butter, softened
1½ cups granulated sugar
2 teaspoons vanilla extract
2 eggs
1¼ cups buttermilk

This deep, dark chocolate cake is so quick and easy to prepare you'll find yourself inventing special occasions just to be able to bake it!

Prep Time: 10 to 15 minutes
Baking Time: 25 to 35 minutes
Equipment: two 9-inch cake pans, measuring spoons, measuring cups, medium bowl, large bowl, electric mixer, spatula, cooling rack, knife

1. Preheat the oven to 350 degrees F. Lightly grease and flour two 9-inch cake pans.
2. In a medium bowl, mix the flour, baking soda, salt, and cocoa. Set aside.
3. In a large bowl, cream the butter, sugar, and vanilla with an electric mixer on medium speed until light and fluffy, about 2 minutes, stopping twice to scrape the bowl and beaters with a spatula.
4. Add the eggs one at a time, beating well after each addition.
5. On low speed, alternate adding one-third of the dry ingredients with half of the buttermilk, mixing for 5 to 10 seconds after each addition. Do not blend each addition in fully before adding the next. When everything has been added, scrape the bowl and beaters and mix until blended and smooth (about 5 seconds). Do not overmix.
6. Divide the batter evenly between the prepared pans and smooth the tops with a spatula. Place the pans on the middle rack of the oven, leaving 2 inches between the pans and the oven walls.

7. Bake for 25 to 35 minutes, or until a toothpick inserted in the center comes out clean and the cakes spring back when lightly touched. Do not wait for the cakes to pull away from the sides.
8. Cool the cakes in their pans on a rack for 15 minutes. Loosen the sides with a thin knife and carefully remove the cake layers. Cool completely on a rack before frosting.

Yield: Serves 12 to 14

VARIATIONS

Chocolate–Chocolate Chip Cake: *Add 1 cup chocolate chips to the batter (after step 5).*

Cupcakes: *Line the muffin tins with paper or foil liners (liners keep the cupcakes moist and make them easy to remove). Fill one-half to two-thirds full. Bake at 350 degrees F for 18 to 23 minutes, or until the tops are firm and a toothpick inserted into the center of a cupcake comes out clean. Cool the cupcakes completely in the tin on a rack. Remove and frost. Makes 24 cupcakes.*

Frosting and Filling: *Be creative with your frostings and fillings. This cake is great with chocolate or vanilla frosting and a fruit filling between layers.*

TIPS

If you're using a 13 by 9 by 2-inch pan, bake for thirty-five to forty-five minutes.

Line the cake pans with lightly greased and floured parchment or waxed paper to prevent sticking.

For slight flavor variations, substitute milk, sour cream, or water for the buttermilk.

Use Magi-Cake Strips around the sides of the pan to prevent the outside crust from overbaking.

Use a heart-shaped pan for Valentine's Day.

Angel Food Cake

಄ ಄

1 cup cake flour
1⅓ cups granulated sugar
¼ teaspoon salt
1½ cups egg whites
(about 12) at room
temperature
1¼ teaspoons cream
of tartar
1 teaspoon vanilla extract

Divinely light and nonfat to boot—it's no wonder this dessert is honored with this heavenly name!

Prep Time: 15 to 20 minutes
Baking Time: 45 to 55 minutes
Equipment: 10-inch tube pan (preferably with a removable bottom and legs), measuring spoons, measuring cups, parchment or waxed paper, sifter or sieve, large bowl, electric mixer, spatula, knife, wine bottle or funnel (for cooling)

1. Preheat the oven to 350 degrees F. Cut a sheet of parchment or waxed paper to fit the bottom of a 10-inch tube pan. Place the paper in the pan.
2. Pour the flour, ⅓ cup of the sugar, and the salt into a sifter or wire strainer placed over waxed or parchment paper. Sift three times, working back and forth between two sheets of paper. Set aside.
3. In a large bowl, beat the egg whites with an electric mixer on low speed until foamy (1 to 1½ minutes). Stop the mixer and sprinkle the cream of tartar on top of the egg whites. Resume mixing, increasing the speed to medium, and beat until soft, droopy peaks form when the beaters are withdrawn. The mixture will look like whipped marshmallow topping. This can take several minutes.
4. Lower the speed to medium-low and add the remaining 1 cup of sugar, 2 tablespoons at a time (make sure there are no lumps in the sugar before adding), beating after each

addition. Keep beating at medium speed until the whites hold peaks that slightly droop at the top. The peaks should still be moist, perfectly smooth, and glossy looking. This can take several minutes.

5. Add the vanilla and beat just to incorporate.

6. Sift about one-quarter of the dry ingredients over the egg whites. Using a spatula or your open and extended fingers, gently fold the dry ingredients into the egg whites just until blended and no streaks of flour show. Repeat three more times until all of the dry ingredients have been incorporated.

7. Hold the bowl close to the ungreased pan and, using a spatula, gently transfer the batter to the cake pan. Gently run a knife or the spatula around the batter to eliminate any large air pockets that may have formed. Smooth the top with the spatula.

8. Bake for 45 to 55 minutes, or until a toothpick inserted into the middle of the cake comes out clean and the cake springs back when lightly touched.

9. Invert the pan on a bottle neck or a funnel so the bottom does not touch the counter. If you're using a pan with feet, just invert. It is important for air to circulate underneath the cake so it cools evenly.

10. Cool the cake completely in the pan. Remove the cake by cutting around the sides and tube with a thin knife, using an up-and-down motion while pressing the knife firmly against the pan. Gently shake the cake onto a plate, tapping the top with the knife a couple of times if necessary. Remove the paper from the top of the cake.

Yield: Serves 10 to 12

(Continues)

Fruity Angel Food Cake: *Serve with fresh strawberries or raspberries mixed with sugar.*

Chocolate Angel Food Cake: *Replace 1/4 cup flour with 1/4 cup unsweetened cocoa.*

Almond Joy: *Substitute almond extract for vanilla.*

Chocolate Glazed: *Drizzle chocolate glaze over the top of cake (see recipe for glaze, page 112).*

Fondue Anyone?: *Cut the cake into pieces and dip it into warm melted chocolate for a festive dessert.*

TIPS

Read "Beating and Folding Egg Whites," page 103, before you begin the recipe.

Sift or strain cream of tartar if it is clumping.

Angel food batter doubles in volume during baking.

A tube pan conducts heat to the center of the cake, cooking the cake from the inside as well as from the outside.

Cooling the angel food cake upside down in its pan helps keep its shape and allows the steam from the cake to condense on the bottom of the pan to prevent sticking.

To keep this cake's airy texture, gently cut it with a serrated knife using a sawing motion.

Sponge Cake

❧ ❦

1 cup all-purpose flour
1 cup granulated sugar
¼ teaspoon salt
6 egg whites, at room temperature
1 teaspoon cream of tartar
6 egg yolks, at room temperature
1 teaspoon vanilla extract

Sponge cake uses both beaten egg whites and yolks for its soft and light texture, but has no butter or added fat. It's great smothered in whipped cream and strawberries.

Prep Time: 15 to 20 minutes
Baking Time: 35 to 45 minutes
Equipment: 10-inch tube pan (preferably with a removable bottom and legs), measuring spoons, measuring cups, parchment or waxed paper, sifter or sieve, large bowl, medium bowl, electric mixer, whisk, spatula, knife, wine bottle or funnel (for cooling)

1. Preheat the oven to 350 degrees F. Cut a sheet of parchment or waxed paper to fit the bottom of a 10-inch tube pan. Place the paper in the pan.
2. Pour the flour, ½ cup of the sugar, and the salt into a sifter or wire strainer placed over waxed or parchment paper. Sift three times, working back and forth between two sheets of paper. Set aside.
3. In a large bowl, beat the egg whites with an electric mixer on low speed until foamy (1 to 1½ minutes). Stop the mixer and sprinkle the cream of tartar on top of the egg whites. Resume mixing, increasing the speed to medium, and beat until soft, droopy peaks form when the beaters are withdrawn. The mixture will look like whipped marshmallow topping. This can take several minutes.
4. Lower the speed to medium-low and add the remaining ½ cup of sugar, 2 tablespoons at a time (make sure there are no lumps in the sugar before adding), beating after each addition. Keep beating at medium speed until the whites

hold peaks that slightly droop at the top. The peaks should still be moist, perfectly smooth, and glossy looking. This can take several minutes.

5. In a medium bowl, beat the egg yolks and vanilla with a whisk until thickened.

6. Pour the egg yolk mixture on top of the whites. Sift the dry ingredients on top of the yolks.

7. Using a spatula or your open and extended fingers, gently fold the egg yolks and flour into the egg whites just until blended and no streaks of yolk or flour show.

8. Hold the bowl close to the ungreased pan and, using a spatula, gently transfer the batter to the cake pan. Smooth the top with the spatula.

9. Bake for 35 to 45 minutes, or until the cake is lightly golden, a toothpick inserted into the middle of the cake comes out clean, and the cake springs back when lightly touched.

10. Invert the pan on a bottle neck or a funnel so the bottom does not touch the counter. If you're using a pan with feet, just invert. It is important for air to circulate underneath the cake so it cools evenly.

11. Cool the cake completely in the pan. Remove the cake by cutting around the sides and tube with a thin knife using an up-and-down motion while pressing the knife firmly against the pan. Gently shake the cake onto a plate, tapping the top with the knife a couple of times if necessary. Remove the paper from the top of the cake.

Yield: Serves 10 to 12

Fruity Sponge Shortcake: *Serve with fresh strawberries or raspberries mixed with sugar and lots of whipped cream.*

Lemon Joy: *Add 2 teaspoons grated lemon zest to the egg yolks for a hint of lemon flavor.*

Chocolate Glazed: *Split the cake into 2 or 3 layers, fill with whipped cream, and top with chocolate glaze (see recipe for glaze, page 112).*

Chocolate Sponge Cake: *Replace $^1/_3$ cup flour with $^1/_3$ cup unsweetened cocoa.*

TIPS

Read "Beating and Folding Egg Whites," page 103, before you begin the recipe.

Sponge cake can also be made in eight- or nine-inch cake pans or in a nine-inch springform pan and split for a layered shortcake.

Sift or strain cream of tartar if it is clumping.

A tube pan conducts heat to the center of the cake, cooking the cake from the inside as well as from the outside.

Cooling the sponge cake upside down in its pan helps keep its shape and allows the steam from the cake to condense on the bottom of the pan to prevent sticking.

To keep this cake's airy texture, gently cut it with a serrated knife using a sawing motion.

Pound Cake

❧ ☙

2 cups all-purpose flour
1 teaspoon baking powder
¼ teaspoon salt
1 cup (2 sticks) butter, softened
1¼ cups granulated sugar
1 teaspoon vanilla extract
4 eggs, room temperature
¼ cup milk, room temperature

This cake got its name because the original recipe called for one pound each of the primary ingredients—flour, butter, sugar, and eggs.

Prep Time: 10 to 15 minutes
Baking Time: 55 to 65 minutes
Equipment: 9 by 5 by 3-inch loaf pan, measuring spoons, measuring cups, spatula, medium bowl, large bowl, electric mixer, spatula, cooling rack, knife

1. Preheat the oven to 325 degrees F. Lightly grease and flour a 9 by 5 by 3-inch loaf pan.
2. In a medium bowl, mix the flour, baking powder, and salt. Set aside.
3. In a large bowl, cream the butter with an electric mixer on medium-high speed for 30 seconds.
4. Add the sugar, 2 tablespoons at a time. Beat until light and fluffy, about 5 minutes, stopping twice to scrape the bowl and beaters with a spatula.
5. Add the vanilla and the eggs one at a time, beating well after each addition. Scrape the bowl and beaters.
6. On low speed, alternate adding half of the dry ingredients with the milk, mixing for 5 to 10 seconds after each addition. When everything has been added, scrape the bowl and beaters and mix on low speed until blended and smooth (about 5 seconds). Do not overmix.
7. Scrape the batter into the prepared pan and smooth the top with a spatula.
8. Bake for 55 to 65 minutes, or until the cake is lightly golden, a toothpick inserted in the center comes out clean, and the

cake springs back when lightly touched. Loosely cover the cake with foil after 30 to 40 minutes to prevent it from over-browning.

9. Cool the cake in its pan on a rack for 15 minutes. Loosen the sides with a thin knife. Remove the cake from the pan and cool thoroughly on a rack.

Yield: Serves 12 to 16

Variations

Chocolate Chip Pound Cake: *Add 1 cup chocolate chips to the batter (after step 6).*

Lemon Pound Cake: *Substitute 1 tablespoon freshly squeezed lemon juice for the vanilla and add 1 tablespoon finely grated lemon zest (step 5).*

Chocolate Marbled Pound Cake: *In a small bowl, reserve one-third of the batter. Mix it with 1 ounce of melted unsweetened chocolate. When you fill the pan, alternate large spoonfuls of regular batter with chocolate batter, and swirl with a knife for a marbleized effect.*

Fruity Pound Cake: *Serve with fresh strawberries or raspberries mixed with sugar and lots of whipped cream.*

Poppy Seed Pound Cake: *Soak 2 tablespoons of poppy seeds in the milk overnight. Add the poppy seeds with the milk.*

Tips

It is important to have the butter, milk, and eggs at room temperature. Otherwise, the batter may separate during mixing and the cake will be less tender.

Traditional pound cake has one-quarter teaspoon mace. For a slightly spiced flavor, add it to the dry ingredients.

Strawberry Shortcake

❧ ❧

Strawberries

2   pints strawberries, cleaned, hulled, and sliced
1/3   cup granulated sugar
8   to 12 whole strawberries, for garnish (optional)

Shortcake

2   cups all-purpose flour
1   tablespoon baking powder
1/4   cup granulated sugar
1/2   teaspoon salt
1/2   cup (1 stick) butter, chilled and cut into large pieces
2/3   cup milk, plus extra for glazing
3   tablespoons butter, softened

Whipped Cream

2   cups heavy cream
3   tablespoons confectioners' sugar
1   teaspoon vanilla extract

The quintessential summertime treat—a base of buttery and tender biscuit topped with lots of whipped cream and fresh strawberries. Make one large cake or individual shortcakes.

Prep Time: 20 to 25 minutes
Baking Time: 20 to 30 minutes
Equipment: 9-inch cake pan, measuring spoons, measuring cups, medium bowl, large bowls, cooling rack, knife, electric mixer (food processor, optional)

1. Preheat the oven to 450 degrees F. Take out a 9-inch cake pan.
2. Prepare the strawberries. In a medium bowl, mix the strawberries and sugar. Set aside.
3. Prepare the shortcake. In a food processor fitted with a metal chopping blade, add the flour, baking powder, sugar, and salt. Pulse to combine (about four pulses).
4. Add the butter and pulse until the mixture resembles coarse crumbs (about ten pulses).
5. Add the milk and pulse until just combined and evenly moistened (about five pulses). Do not allow the dough to form a ball.
6. Transfer the dough to a lightly floured surface. Knead for about 30 seconds, pushing the dough with the palms of your hands, to make the dough less sticky.
7. Pat the dough into the ungreased cake pan and brush the top with milk.
8. Bake for 20 to 30 minutes, or until the shortcake is golden and the top is firm.

9. Cool the cake in its pan on a rack for 10 minutes. Loosen the sides with a thin knife and carefully remove and split the cake into 2 layers. Spread softened butter on the cut sides.

10. Just before serving, prepare the whipped cream. In a large bowl, with an electric mixer on medium-high speed, whip the cream to soft peaks. Add the sugar and vanilla and beat until stiff peaks form. Do not overbeat.

11. Place the bottom of the shortcake, cut side up, on a serving plate. Top with half the strawberries and half the whipped cream. Place the remaining shortcake on top, cut side down. Top with the remaining strawberries and whipped cream. Garnish with whole strawberries.

Yield: serves 8 to 10

VARIATIONS

Individual Shortcakes: *For individual shortcakes, pat or gently roll the dough $^1/_2$ inch thick. Using lightly floured 3-inch cutters or a knife, cut out shortcakes (press scraps together for additional shortcakes). Transfer the shortcakes to an ungreased baking sheet and brush the tops with milk. Bake 13 to 18 minutes, or until golden and the tops are firm. For easier to split individual shortcakes, roll the dough $^1/_4$ inch thick and fold in half before cutting.*

July Fourth Special: *Top the shortcakes with a combination of strawberries and blueberries for a red, white, and blue celebration.*

Tutti-Frutti Shortcakes: *Substitute peaches, nectarines, or raspberries for the strawberries, or use a combination of fruit.*

TIPS

Shortcake can also be made easily by hand. Combine the dry ingredients in bowl. Add the butter and work the mixture with your fingertips until it resembles coarse crumbs. Add the milk and stir gently until just combined. Continue with step 6.

You can also make the shortcake in an eight-inch cake pan or a springform pan.

A large freeform shortcake can be baked on a baking sheet.

If you don't have a rolling pin or cutters, you can drop individual shortcakes from a large spoon onto a baking sheet.

For easier whipping, chill the bowl and the beaters before beating the cream.

Whip the cream only until firm peaks form, or you will end up with butter.

Whip the cream as close to the serving time as possible. It will deflate if left for a long time in the refrigerator.

Coffee Cake

Streusel

1   cup walnuts or pecans (optional)

½   cup all-purpose flour

¼   cup brown sugar, firmly packed

2   teaspoons ground cinnamon

¼   cup (½ stick) butter, softened and cut into large pieces

Cake

2   cups all-purpose flour

1½   teaspoons baking powder

1   teaspoons baking soda

¼   teaspoon salt

¾   cup (1½ sticks) butter, softened

1   cup granulated sugar

1   tablespoon vanilla extract

2   eggs

1   cup sour cream

Topped and layered with a crunchy brown sugar and nut streusel, this coffee cake is not just for mornings and tastes great with a lot more than just coffee.

Prep Time: 15 to 20 minutes

Baking Time: 55 to 65 minutes

Equipment: 9-inch springform pan, measuring spoons, measuring cups, medium bowl, large bowl, electric mixer, spatula, cooling rack, knife (food processor, optional)

1. Preheat the oven to 350 degrees F. Lightly grease a 9-inch springform pan.
2. Prepare the streusel. In a food processor fitted with a metal chopping blade, pulse the nuts until coarsely chopped. Add the flour, brown sugar, and cinnamon, and pulse five times. Add the butter and pulse briefly until the mixture is coarse and crumbly. Remove ¾ cup and set aside. Pulse the remaining mixture until well moistened. Reserve separately.
3. Prepare the cake. In a medium bowl, mix the flour, baking powder, baking soda, and salt. Set aside.
4. In a large bowl, cream the butter, sugar, and vanilla with an electric mixer on medium speed until light and fluffy, about 2 minutes, stopping twice to scrape the bowl and beaters with a spatula.

(Continues)

5. Add the eggs one at a time, beating well after each addition.
6. On low speed, alternate adding one-third of the dry ingredients with half of the sour cream, mixing for 5 to 10 seconds after each addition. Do not blend each addition in fully before adding the next. When everything has been added, scrape the bowl and beaters and mix until blended and smooth (about 5 seconds). Do not overmix. The batter will be very thick.
7. Spread half of the batter in the prepared pan. Sprinkle the ¾ cup of streusel mixture evenly over the batter. Add the remaining batter. Using a spatula or your fingertips, top with the reserved streusel, distributing evenly.
8. Bake for 55 to 65 minutes, or until a toothpick inserted in the center comes out clean. Do not wait for the cake to pull away from the sides. Loosely cover the cake with aluminum foil after 40 minutes to prevent the topping from overbrowning.
9. Cool the cake in its pan on a rack for 15 minutes. Loosen the sides with a thin knife and carefully remove the sides of the springform pan. Serve warm or at room temperature.

Yield: Serves 10 to 12

VARIATIONS

Hidden Apple Treat: *Peel, core, and thinly slice a large Granny Smith apple (it should be just over 1 cup) and sprinkle with 2 teaspoons fresh lemon juice. Place the apples on top of the inside layer of streusel for a hidden and delicious surprise.*

Chocolate Chip Coffee Cake: *Omit the streusel. Add 1 1/2 cups chocolate chips to the batter (after step 6). Top with a mixture of 3 tablespoons sugar and 1 teaspoon cinnamon. This can also be made in a Bundt pan.*

TIPS

A springform pan allows you to bake a topped coffee cake "right side up" and easily remove it from its pan. Make sure the sides and the base of the springform pan fit together securely.

You can bake this cake in a nine-inch-square pan, but it would be difficult to transfer the whole cake to a serving dish. Cut and serve the cake from the pan.

If you're preparing the streusel by hand, coarsely chop the nuts before mixing.

Use Magi-Cake Strips around the sides of the pan to prevent the outside crust from overbaking.

Frozen coffee cake is better if reheated before serving. Reheat a thawed cake for fifteen minutes in a 350-degree-F oven.

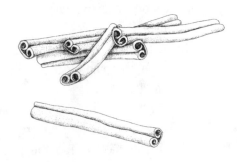

Cheesecake

❧ ☙

Crust

1¼ cups graham cracker
    crumbs (about 10
    large crackers)
¼   cup (½ stick) butter,
    melted
2   tablespoons sugar

Cheesecake Filling

24 ounces cream cheese,
    softened
1   cup granulated sugar
1   cup sour cream
3   eggs
1   teaspoon vanilla extract

Who doesn't love creamy cheesecake? Because it needs time to chill, it's the perfect make-ahead dessert.

Prep Time: 15 to 20 minutes, plus 3 hours to chill
Baking Time: 55 to 65 minutes
Equipment: 9-inch springform pan, measuring spoons, measuring cups, medium bowl or food processor, large bowl, electric mixer, spatula, cooling rack, knife

1. Preheat the oven to 375 degrees F. Take out a 9-inch springform pan.
2. Prepare the crust. In a food processor or medium bowl, combine the crumbs, butter, and sugar. Blend until moistened and smooth. Press the crust evenly into the bottom of a 9-inch springform pan. Refrigerate while you prepare the filling.
3. Prepare the filling. In a large bowl, beat the cream cheese with an electric mixer on medium-low speed, until very smooth, stopping twice to scrape the bowl and beaters with a spatula.
4. On low speed, add the sugar and sour cream. Beat until combined, stopping twice to scrape the bowl and beaters with a spatula.
5. Add the eggs and the vanilla, and mix until blended.
6. Pour the filling into the crust-lined pan, and smooth the top with a spatula. Tap the pan three or four times on the counter to eliminate air bubbles.

7. Bake for 55 to 65 minutes, or until the cheesecake looks set around the edges and the center appears nearly set. The center may jiggle slightly when you gently shake the pan. The cake will become firm as it cools.

8. Cool the cake in its pan on a rack for 15 minutes. Run the tip of a knife gently around the cake to loosen it from the pan while the cake is still warm. This will prevent the top from cracking as the cake cools and contracts from the sides of the pan. Let the cake cool completely before removing the sides of the pan.

9. Chill the cheesecake until it's cold and firm, at least 3 hours. Remove it from the refrigerator 20 to 30 minutes before serving.

Yield: Serves 10 to 12

VARIATIONS

Crust Crazy: *For variety, experiment with different cookie crumbs for the crust. Substitute Oreos, chocolate wafers, vanilla wafers, coconut macaroons, gingersnaps, peanut butter cookies, or chocolate chip cookies for graham crackers. Omit the added sugar when using sweeter cookies.*

Chocolate Marble: *In a small bowl, reserve $1/3$ of the batter. Mix it with 2 ounces melted unsweetened chocolate. When you fill the pan, alternate large spoonfuls of regular batter with chocolate batter and swirl with a knife for a marbleized effect.*

Tutti-Frutti: *Top the baked cheesecake with whole strawberries or other fresh fruit.*

Easy Topping: *Combine $3/4$ cup sour cream, 1 tablespoon sugar, and $1/2$ teaspoon vanilla in a small bowl and whisk until smooth. Spread the mixture evenly over the top of the baked cheesecake. This hides any imperfections and tastes great.*

July Fourth Special: *Top the baked cheesecake with strawberries or raspberries and blueberries for a special red, white, and blue dessert.*

Chocolate Chip Cheesecake: *Make a chocolate crust: substitute crushed chocolate wafers for the graham crackers and eliminate the sugar. Add 1 cup semisweet chocolate chips to the batter and sprinkle $1/2$ cup semisweet chocolate chips on top of the cake before baking.*

Lemon Cheesecake: *Stir 3 tablespoons freshly squeezed lemon juice and 1 teaspoon grated lemon zest into the batter (step 4).*

Pumpkin Cheesecake: *Mix $1/2$ cup canned pumpkin, $1/2$ teaspoon cinnamon, a pinch of cloves, and a pinch of nutmeg into the cream cheese (step 3). Flavor the graham cracker crust with $1/2$ teaspoon cinnamon, ginger, nutmeg, or allspice.*

TIPS

A springform pan, consisting of a base that fits into a metal ring with a spring release, allows you to bake a cheesecake "right side up." Make sure the sides and the base of the springform pan fit together securely.

Take the cream cheese out of the refrigerator an hour before starting the recipe to allow it to come to room temperature, or microwave it on high—fifteen seconds for each eight-ounce unwrapped package.

Make sure all ingredients are at room temperature and mix only until smooth. If a cheesecake has too much air beaten into the batter it can collapse when cooling, creating a crater in the center of the cake.

Cheesecake batter can also be made in a food processor fitted with a metal chopping blade.

For attractive presentation and to prevent leakage of the cheesecake batter, press the crust at least one inch up the sides of the pan.

Don't open the oven door during early baking or the cake could fall or crack.

Avoid overbaking. Residual heat will continue to cook the cheesecake. It becomes firm only after it is cooled.

It is normal for the top of the cheesecake to crack. Hide imperfections with fruit or sour cream topping.

Cheesecakes can be made twenty-four to thirty-six hours before serving time.

If the cake sticks to the sides of the springform pan when releasing it, wrap a damp, hot cotton towel around sides of pan, covering it completely, and hold in place for one minute.

If you plan to travel with the cake, line the bottom of the pan with parchment paper so you can remove the springform disk.

To easily cut the cheesecake, heat the blade of a serrated knife or server under hot running water and wipe dry before cutting each slice.

For optimum flavor, do not freeze longer than one month.

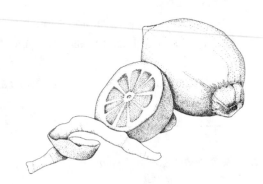

Vanilla Frosting

3¾ cups (1 pound) con-
     fectioners' sugar
½ cup (1 stick) butter,
     softened
2 teaspoons vanilla
     extract
¼ cup milk
     (approximately)

This white, creamy frosting is great with chocolate or yellow layer cakes.

Prep Time: 5 to 10 minutes
Equipment: measuring spoons, measuring cups, sifter or wire strainer, medium bowl, large bowl, electric mixer, spatula

1. Pour the confectioners' sugar (1 cup at a time) into a sifter or wire strainer placed over a medium bowl.
2. In a large bowl, cream the butter with an electric mixer on medium speed until light and fluffy, about 1 minute.
3. Gradually add half of the sugar and beat well.
4. Add the vanilla and half of the milk. The mixture will be dry and crumbly.
5. Add the rest of the sugar and enough milk for desired spreading consistency. Beat on high until smooth.

Yield: Frosts one 8- or 9-inch two-layer cake or 24 cupcakes

VARIATIONS

Lemon Frosting: *Omit the vanilla, substitute freshly squeezed lemon juice for the milk, and add 2 teaspoons grated lemon zest.*

Orange Frosting: *Omit the vanilla, substitute freshly squeezed orange juice for the milk, and add 1 tablespoon grated orange zest.*

Peanut Butter Frosting: *Substitute peanut butter for the butter.*

Coffee Frosting: *Dissolve 2 teaspoons instant coffee into warm milk.*

Coconut Frosting: *Spread 1 1/2 cups sweetened shredded coconut on a baking sheet and bake at 350 degrees F for about 7 to 12 minutes, or until just golden. Shake the pan periodically for even browning. Cool. Sprinkle toasted coconut on top of the frosting.*

Fruity Fillings: *Use jams as fillings or mix melted jam with frosting for a fruity flavor.*

TIPS

Sifting or straining the sugar eliminates lumps in the final frosting.

For a smooth frosting, make sure to beat it well.

To prevent runny frosting, use only enough milk to achieve the right spreading consistency.

Chocolate Frosting

❦ ❧

3¾ cups (1 pound) confec-
    tioners' sugar
½ cup unsweetened cocoa
½ cup (1 stick) butter, soft-
    ened
1 teaspoon vanilla extract
⅓ cup milk
    (approximately)

A perfect chocolate complement to any layer cake or cupcake.

Prep Time: 5 to 10 minutes
Equipment: measuring spoons, measuring cups, sifter or wire strainer, medium bowl, large bowl, electric mixer, spatula

1. Pour the confectioners' sugar (1 cup at a time) and cocoa into a sifter or wire strainer placed over a medium bowl. Mix until blended.
2. In a large bowl, cream the butter with an electric mixer on medium speed until light and fluffy, about 1 minute.
3. Gradually add half of the dry ingredients and beat well.
4. Add the vanilla and half of the milk. The mixture will be dry and crumbly.
5. Add the rest of the dry ingredients and enough milk for desired spreading consistency. Beat on high until smooth.

Yield: Frosts one 8- or 9-inch two-layer cake or 24 cupcakes

VARIATIONS

Mocha Frosting: *Warm the milk and stir in 1 tablespoon instant coffee.*

Chocolate Cherry Frosting: *Stir 3 tablespoons drained and chopped maraschino cherries into the frosting.*

Chocolate–Peanut Butter Frosting: *Substitute peanut butter for the butter.*

TIPS

Sifting or straining the sugar and cocoa eliminates lumps in the final frosting.

For a smooth frosting, make sure to beat it well.

To prevent runny frosting, use only enough milk to achieve the right spreading consistency.

The First Book of Baking

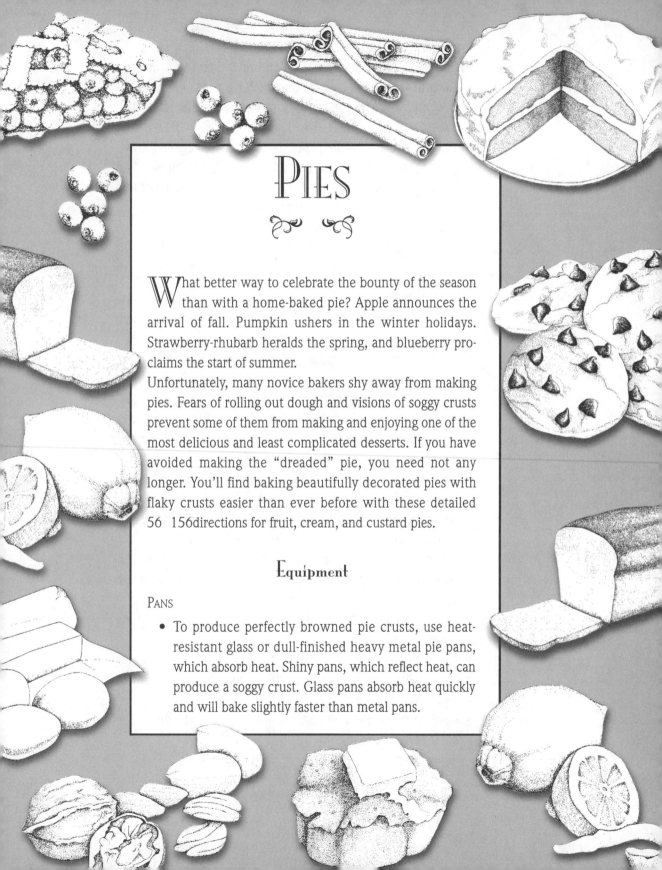

PIES

❧ ❧

What better way to celebrate the bounty of the season than with a home-baked pie? Apple announces the arrival of fall. Pumpkin ushers in the winter holidays. Strawberry-rhubarb heralds the spring, and blueberry proclaims the start of summer.

Unfortunately, many novice bakers shy away from making pies. Fears of rolling out dough and visions of soggy crusts prevent some of them from making and enjoying one of the most delicious and least complicated desserts. If you have avoided making the "dreaded" pie, you need not any longer. You'll find baking beautifully decorated pies with flaky crusts easier than ever before with these detailed 56   156directions for fruit, cream, and custard pies.

Equipment

PANS

- To produce perfectly browned pie crusts, use heat-resistant glass or dull-finished heavy metal pie pans, which absorb heat. Shiny pans, which reflect heat, can produce a soggy crust. Glass pans absorb heat quickly and will bake slightly faster than metal pans.

- Use the size pie pan listed in the recipe so the crust and filling fit. This book calls for nine-inch pie pans. To check the size, measure the pan across the top inside diameter with a ruler.
- You can use disposable pie pans, but they have some drawbacks. Their light weight makes it difficult to get them in and out of the oven. Also, some disposable pans are smaller and more shallow than the standard size pie pans. Check the size and adjust the recipe accordingly.

OTHER EQUIPMENT

- A food processor fitted with a metal chopping blade quickly combines pie crust ingredients. Use the pulse button for control so the dough isn't overworked.
- To mix pie dough manually, use a pastry blender, a knife, or your fingertips. Don't work the dough with warm hands—the butter will melt and the crust won't be flaky.
- A pastry blender—a wooden handle attached to six heavy wires bent in a half-circle—allows you to easily cut fat and flour together.
- Your rolling pin should fit comfortably in your hands. If you don't have a rolling pin, use a wine bottle (it can even be filled with cold water to help keep the dough chilled as long as condensation doesn't form).
- Wood, Formica, or marble countertops make good rolling surfaces. Make sure the surface is large enough to roll the dough a few inches larger than your pie pan.
- A long metal spatula or dough scraper is useful for lifting dough off the rolling surface.
- Use a sturdy mixing spoon or spatula to combine fruit fillings.
- Use a sturdy mixing spoon or whisk to combine custard or cream fillings.
- Cooling racks allow air to circulate freely on all sides of the pie for proper cooling.

Ingredients

- Use either bleached or unbleached all-purpose flour for pie crusts.
- Unsalted butter is recommended for flavorful and flaky pie crusts. Do not substitute margarine for butter in pie crusts.
- To substitute vegetable shortening or lard for butter in a pie crust, use 15 percent less. Vegetable shortening and lard have a higher fat content than butter (butter is about 80 to 85 percent fat).
- Use in-season fruit that is ripe and flavorful.
- Use fresh dairy products.
- Use pure, not imitation, extracts.
- Use fresh and fragrant spices.

Easy as Pie

MIXING PIE DOUGH

- Pie crust dough is actually tiny layers of chilled butter coated with flour and held together by a small amount of liquid. The crust's flakiness is created when the solid chunks of butter melt and the liquid in the dough converts to steam and expands within the dough, creating air pockets in the cooked crust. If the dough is overworked and the butter becomes incorporated into the dough, the crust will lose its airiness and be tough and mealy instead of light and flaky.
- To make light, flaky pie dough, remember these important rules: Keep the ingredients cold, blend the fat and flour properly, add only as much liquid as necessary, and handle the dough as little as possible.
- To keep the ingredients cool, put the flour and salt in a zip-top bag in the freezer an hour before baking, keep the butter in the refrigerator until ready to use, and put ice cubes in the water.

- Cut in the butter only until it is evenly distributed and the dough looks like coarse meal. It should not appear oily.
- Sprinkle the water over the flour mixture instead of pouring it all in one spot. Use enough water to moisten the dough. Too much water will make the pastry tough, but too little will make it dry, brittle, and difficult to roll out.
- When using a food processor to mix ingredients, stop the machine after the dough begins to clump together but before it becomes a single ball. The dough should only form a solid mass when pressed together.
- After mixing, scrape the dough out onto a work surface. Form the mixture into one ball for a single-crust pie, or two balls for a double-crust pie or two single-crust pies. The dough should feel soft and velvety. Flatten the dough to a one-inch-thick disk and wrap well in plastic.
- If the dough is too dry to hold together, return it to the bowl and break it apart. Add water, a few drops at a time, and mix until distributed. Turn it out from the bowl to the work surface and re-form into a ball.
- Refrigerate the dough for thirty to sixty minutes, or until it is firm enough to roll.
- Chilling the dough before rolling allows the gluten to relax, makes the dough more tender, and prevents it from shrinking as it bakes. Chilling also makes the dough less sticky and easier to roll.
- Pie dough can be refrigerated for about three days or frozen for several months if tightly wrapped. Let the dough thaw in the refrigerator, then let it stand at room temperature thirty minutes before rolling it out.

ROLLING PIE DOUGH

- If chilled dough is very firm, let it soften before rolling. The dough must be malleable enough to roll easily or it will crack.

- Roll the dough out on a work space several inches larger than your pan.
- To prevent sticking, lightly dust the rolling surface, rolling pin, and pie dough with flour before rolling. Keep extra flour nearby, but use it sparingly.
- If you are concerned about the dough sticking to the work surface, roll it out between two sheets of lightly floured waxed paper, parchment paper, or plastic wrap. It will probably be necessary to overlap pieces of paper or wrap to accommodate the size of the finished crust. Continually flip the dough during rolling and pull off one side of the paper or plastic and then reattach it. This frees the dough, making it stick less and stretch more.
- If you're using a pastry cloth and a rolling pin cover, lightly sprinkle the cloth and the cover with flour before rolling.
- Using a light touch, roll the dough in one direction at a time from the center of the dough out to the edge. Do not roll back and forth over the entire surface.
- Turn the dough over one or two times during rolling to prevent sticking (dust very lightly with flour if necessary).
- After every couple of rolls, pick up the dough and rotate it forty-five degrees to stop it from sticking and to maintain a comfortable rolling angle. If necessary, use a pastry scraper or a long metal spatula to free the dough from the rolling surface before turning.
- If the dough begins to stick to the rolling pin or the rolling surface, lightly reapply flour.
- If the edges begin to crack, pinch them together with a little water before the cracks deepen. If larger cracks form, cut a piece from the edge of the dough, moisten, and patch the hole.
- During rolling, try to keep the shape of the dough as circular as possible, pressing evenly with both hands to maintain a uniform thickness.

- To prevent the edges from becoming too thin, don't roll over them. When the rolling pin approaches the edge of the dough, lift it up instead of rolling over the edge.
- If bits of dough stick to the rolling pin, remove them before they tear the dough.
- Rolled dough should be between one-sixteenth and one-eighth inch thick. An easy way to measure the thickness of rolled dough is to mark the desired thickness on a toothpick and then insert it into the dough to gauge the depth.
- Finished crusts should be about two inches larger than the top of the pie pan to allow for trimming and shrinkage. An easy way to measure the width is to lay the pie pan upside-down on the dough and cut a circle one inch wider than the pan.

FITTING THE DOUGH IN THE PAN

- Always brush off any excess flour before transferring the dough to the pie pan.
- To transfer the bottom crust to the pie pan, drape the pastry over the rolling pin, unroll it into the pie pan, and ease the dough into the pan without stretching. Press the dough against the pan to prevent air pockets and shrinkage. Another method is to fold the dough in half or in quarters, center it in the pan, and unfold.
- Do not try to stretch the dough to fit in the pan. It will shrink during baking.
- If the dough cracks or tears when you're fitting it in the pie pan, patch it with trimmings. If you don't, the crust will absorb the filling and get soft.

STORING AND DEFROSTING PIE DOUGH

- To freeze rolled and trimmed dough, wrap it tightly and stack it in rounds between layers of lightly floured waxed paper or foil, protected by a stiff piece of cardboard so it holds its shape.

- Defrost rolled dough with the plastic wrap on the pastry so condensation will form on the plastic, not on the dough. Rolled dough only takes a few minutes to defrost before it can fit into a pie pan.
- Unbaked pie shells can be kept in the refrigerator for about three days, or can be frozen for several months if tightly wrapped. There is no need to thaw the shell before baking.

DECORATING THE CRUST

- Save excess pie dough to use as decorations.
- A cake turntable is useful for trimming and decorating pie crusts.
- Lightly flour your fingertips if the dough becomes sticky during decorating.

Decorating a Single Crust

- Trim the bottom crust with kitchen shears or a sharp knife, leaving a three-quarters-inch overhang.
- *For a simple pie crust:* Fold the overhang under itself, as if making a hem, so it creates a double thickness even with the edge of the pan, then gently press it onto the rim of the pie pan to seal. This double layer of dough will not dry out or burn as easily as a single layer.
- *For the easiest decoration:* Press the back of the tines of a fork around the rim of the crust. Create different patterns by varying the spacing of the indent marks. Lightly flour the fork if it begins to stick.
- When shaping crust with a decorative border, first tuck the overhang under itself, then pinch the thickened dough so the edge stands up around the rim. This makes it easier to decorate and extends the capacity of the crust so there is less risk of the filling overflowing.
- *To flute (zigzag) the edge:* Place your left forefinger on the inside of the pastry rim. With the thumb and forefinger of your

right hand, push the pastry from the outside of the pan toward your left forefinger, forming a V-shape in the dough. Continue around the edge of the pan, forming a slightly raised zigzag pattern. If it is more comfortable, reverse this motion so your index finger is on the outside edge and the thumb and other index finger are on the inside edge. Use your knuckles if you have long fingernails.

- *For a turret edge:* Fold the overhang underneath itself and pinch to create a slightly raised edge. Cut through the pastry to the rim at half-inch intervals. Press alternate strips of pastry flat around the edge, leaving the others standing up, to give a turret effect.

- *For a starburst edge:* Trim the dough even with the rim of the pan. Cut the edge of the crust at half-inch intervals, making each cut a half-inch long. Fold each piece in half diagonally to form a triangle and press lightly to seal the dough.

- *For a rope or pinched-edge design:* Fold the overhang underneath itself and pinch to create a slightly raised edge. Pinch a small piece of the dough between your thumb and the lower knuckle of your index finger, positioning your hand at a forty-five-degree angle. Slightly roll your index finger toward the inside of the pan to create a diagonal ridge. Repeat this pinching motion around the edge of the crust, putting your index finger in the depression your thumb has just made.

- *To spoon-scallop the crust:* Trim the dough even with the outer edge of the pan. Press the rounded tip of a spoon, face down, around the edge of the crust at close intervals, pressing down to detach the semicircle formed by the spoon's edges. It will look as if little rays are emanating from the crust.

- *For a decorative cut-and-paste border:* Cut different shapes from leftover dough and adhere them to the rim with water, overlapping shapes slightly. If you're making leaves, use a knife to draw veins.

- *For a braided edge:* Cut strips of pastry one-quarter inch wide, braid, place around the crust, and adhere with water.

- Make sure the crust is high enough to contain all the filling so juices don't spill over.
- Pie dough can be used to make free-form tarts or crostadas. Adjust filling and baking time for smaller amounts of filling.

Decorating a Double Crust

- When making a solid-topped double-crust pie, moisten the edge of the bottom crust with a little water, beaten egg yolk, or milk before pressing the top and bottom edges together. This keeps the top firmly attached to the bottom crust.
- *For a solid-topped double-crust pie:* Trim the bottom pastry even with the pan edge. After adding the filling, center the top crust over the pie pan and fold the top crust overhang around the underside of the bottom crust (like tucking in a sheet around a mattress). Alternatively, leave a three-quarter-inch overhang on the top and bottom crusts, press the two crusts together, and turn the overhang underneath itself. Gently press it onto the rim to seal the pie to prevent juices from leaking out and to create a slightly raised ridge. If desired, flute as described for single-crust pies. Cut several one-inch slashes in the middle of the top crust to release steam and prevent a soggy pie. Decorative vent holes can be made using small decorative cutters.
- *For a "woven" lattice top:* Roll out the top crust to a generous one-eighth-inch thickness for easier handling. With a fluted pastry wheel, a sharp knife, or a pizza cutter, cut one-half- to three-quarter-inch wide strips, using a ruler as a guide. Place half the strips about one-and-a-half inches apart in the same direction across the pie filling. Do not seal the ends. Fold every other strip back halfway onto itself. Place the center cross-strip on the pie and unfold the pastry strips. Fold back alternate strips and place the second cross-strip in place. Repeat

to "weave" the lattice. When completed, trim the strips, moisten, seal, and fold all ends under the bottom crust.

- *For an easier crisscross crust:* Roll and cut as described above. Lay half of the strips in one direction parallel to each other, using the longest ones for the center of the pie. Then lay the rest of the strips perpendicular to the other strips to form diamonds or squares.
- To avoid getting filling on the crust, weave the strips on lightly floured waxed paper or foil and then invert them onto the pie.
- Lattice strips can also be twisted to form a spiral before placing on pie. Cut these strips slightly longer than for plain lattice.
- Instead of using a top crust, any fruit pie can be topped with a streusel mixture of one cup flour, one-half cup cold butter, and one-half cup brown sugar, blended until crumbly (one-half cup of oats or nuts can also be added). If you're using a crumb topping, do not dot the fruit with butter.
- While preparing the filling and preheating the oven, refrigerate or freeze the unbaked decorated crust in its pan. The top crust can be refrigerated on top of a waxed paper–covered plate or baking sheet.

Baking

- Prepare the oven. Bake pies on the middle or lower oven rack for well-cooked bottoms and the best heat circulation. If you're baking more than one pie at a time, leave two inches between the pies and the sides of the oven to let air circulate.
- Always preheat the oven for at least fifteen minutes before baking.
- Many single-crust pie shells are partially baked before adding the filling (to keep them crisp) or fully baked (when the fillings don't require baking). Baking a crust without a filling is known as "blind-baking."

- When blind-baking, prick the bottom and sides of the pastry repeatedly with a fork so steam can escape. This prevents air bubbles from forming and puffing up the crust. Cover the dough with lightly oiled foil (shiny side down) and weigh down the foil-covered dough with pie weights, rice, or beans, or fit another pie pan on top of the foil so it will keep its shape during baking. Copper pennies and other coins make great pie weights because they conduct heat. Place enough loose change on top of the foil to hold down the crust.
- Beans or rice that have been used as pie weights can be stored and reused as weights. Do not use them in cooking.
- To repair a pie crust that has cracked during blind-baking, put a scrap of raw dough over the crack—it will cook during the final baking.
- If a piece of crust breaks off, "glue" it together with softened butter. Brush off any excess butter and refrigerate the crust for a few minutes, or until the butter has hardened.
- When baking a pie with its filling, do not prick the pastry.
- To prevent the bottom crust from becoming soggy, brush it lightly with a beaten egg white before baking.
- When making a pie with a liquid filling, set the empty pie shell on the oven rack and transfer the filling to the shell with a pitcher to eliminate the risk of spills from the counter to the oven.
- For nicely finished pie crusts, apply a glaze before baking. Use a beaten egg yolk for a dark finish, a beaten whole egg for a medium finish, an egg and water mixture for a light finish, or a beaten egg white for a clear shine. A sprinkling of sugar also adds a finished look.
- Many pies are baked first at a higher temperature to color and crisp the crust, then at a lower temperature to prevent burning.
- To help the bottom crust brown, place the pie pan on a pre-heated baking sheet.

- A pie crust is done when its surface appears dull, slightly blistered, and golden brown.
- Watch pies during the final fifteen minutes of baking to check for overbrowning and to make sure that the filling isn't bubbling out of the crust.
- To prevent excessive browning of the pie crust or edges, loosely cover a double-crust pie with foil (shiny side up to deflect heat) for the last twenty minutes of baking or when the crust appears to be golden brown.
- To shield a single-crust pie, cut a twelve-inch piece of aluminum foil and make a seven-inch hole in the middle. Lay it over the top of the pie, covering the edges but leaving the center exposed. This shield can be reused. Alternatively, cut strips of foil and place them over the edges.
- If the filling seems done before the crust has browned, slide a foil-lined baking sheet under the pie to catch the drippings. Sprinkle salt on spilled pie juices to prevent them from smoking.
- Allow pies to cool on a rack.

STORING AND FREEZING

- For optimum crispness and freshness, pies should be eaten the day they are baked.
- Baked pie shells can be frozen, tightly wrapped, for four to six months. Baked shells are fragile, so store them carefully.
- Fruit pies can be stored, loosely wrapped, at room temperature. Custard and cream pies (or any pies with a milk- or egg-based filling) should be refrigerated until one-half hour before serving.
- Baked pies can be frozen in their pans for about six months. Before freezing, make sure the pie has cooled completely, then wrap tightly.

- Defrost baked fruit pies unwrapped, at room temperature, for several hours, then recrisp in a preheated 350-degree-F oven for fifteen minutes.
- Defrost custard pies in the refrigerator.
- Unbaked fruit pies can be frozen for several months if well wrapped. Do not defrost before baking, but add fifteen to twenty minutes to the baking time. Fruit pies that have been frozen before baking often have soggier crusts than those frozen after baking. It often helps to add a couple of table-spoons of thickener (flour or cornstarch) to the filling if you're planning to freeze the pie before baking.
- When freezing unbaked pies, don't glaze the crust or cut steam vents. You can glaze the pie before baking, and cut vents after ten minutes of baking.

Pie Crust

Single Crust

1¼ cups all-purpose flour
¼ teaspoon salt
½ cup (1 stick) unsalted butter, chilled and cut into large pieces
2 to 4 tablespoons water, iced

Double Crust

2½ cups all-purpose flour
½ teaspoon salt
1 cup (2 sticks) unsalted butter, chilled and cut into large pieces
5 to 8 tablespoons water, iced

This flaky and tender pie crust is easy to make in a food processor.

Prep Time: 5 to 10 minutes
Equipment: measuring spoons, measuring cups, rolling pin, rolling surface, food processor

1. In food processor fitted with metal chopping blade, mix the flour and salt (about five seconds).
2. Add the butter and pulse until the mixture resembles coarse meal (about ten short pulses).
3. Sprinkle the minimum amount of water over the mixture and pulse until distributed throughout the dough and the crumbs start sticking together (five to ten pulses). Process just until the dough begins to hold together. Test by pinching a piece of dough between your thumb and index fingers. If the crumbs are dry, crack, and don't stick together, add 1 to 2 table-spoons more water (a teaspoon at a time, pulsing three to five times to distribute) until the consistency is right. Do not allow the dough to form a ball.
4. Scrape the dough onto a work surface. Shape the dough into 1 ball for a single crust or 2 balls for a double crust. Flatten the dough into 1-inch-thick disk(s). Wrap the dough tightly with plastic wrap and refrigerate for 30 minutes, or until it is firm enough to roll out.

Yield: One 9-inch single crust or one 9-inch double crust

Flavored Dough: *Experiment with adding different flavorings to dough. For a double crust, add any of these flavorings or a combination of them to the dry ingredients: 1 teaspoon cinnamon, $1/2$ teaspoon of nutmeg or cloves, 1 tablespoon peeled and grated fresh ginger, 1 tablespoon grated orange or lemon zest, $1/2$ cup finely chopped nuts, $1/2$ cup shredded sweetened coconut. (Halve the amounts for a single crust.) You can also substitute fresh fruit juice for half of the water.*

Whole Wheat Dough: *Replace $1/2$ cup of the all-purpose flour with $1/2$ cup whole wheat flour for single crust, or replace 1 cup of the all-purpose flour with 1 cup whole wheat flour for double crust.*

Sweet Dough: *For a slightly sweeter dough, add 2 tablespoons sugar to the dry ingredients.*

TIPS

This recipe makes enough dough so that some is left over for decorating the border.

Crust can also be made using a pastry cutter or a fork. Combine the dry ingredients in a large bowl. Cut in pieces of butter with a knife or a pastry cutter until coarse flakes form. Distribute the water evenly over the mixture and toss with a fork until it begins to clump together. Continue with step 4.

As water is mixed in and the dough begins to hold together, the crumbs will become larger. This will help you gauge if more water is necessary.

Do not process longer than a total of thirty seconds.

Some bakers believe your hands should never touch the dough. They turn the dough from the bowl directly onto the plastic wrap and, using the wrap rather than their fingers, press the dough into a ball and flatten.

If you do not have unsalted butter, you can use salted butter.

Do not substitute margarine for butter.

If you are avoiding animal fats, replace the butter with three-quarters cup of chilled solid vegetable shortening for a double crust or six tablespoons for a single crust.

Cookie Crusts

1½ cups cookie crumbs
¼ cup (½ stick) butter, melted
2 tablespoons sugar

Easy-to-make cookie crusts are a great alternative to pastry crusts.

Prep Time: 5 to 10 minutes
Equipment: 9-inch pie pan, measuring spoons, measuring cups, food processor or medium bowl

1. Combine the crumbs, butter, and sugar in a food processor or medium bowl. Blend until moistened and smooth.
2. Press the crust evenly into the bottom of a 9-inch pie pan.
3. Refrigerate while preparing the filling, or bake for 5 to 8 minutes at 350 degrees F for a toasted flavor.

Yield: 1 single pie crust

VARIATION

Crust Crazy: *Use graham crackers, chocolate wafers, vanilla wafers, Oreos, coconut macaroons, gingersnaps, peanut butter cookies, or chocolate chip cookies for variety.*

TIPS

One-and-one-half cups of cookie crumbs equals about twelve large graham crackers, thirty chocolate wafers, or fifteen Oreos.

If you do not have a food processor, put the cookies in a plastic bag and roll over them with a rolling pin or crush them with a hammer.

The First Book of Baking

Apple Pie

Pastry for 9-inch double-crust pie (see recipe, page 160)

The classic American dessert—flaky pastry containing a bounty of delicately spiced apples. Whether you serve it plain or à la mode, there's nothing like an apple pie as good as Mom's.

Filling

6	cups apples, peeled, cored, and thinly sliced (about 6 medium apples)
1	tablespoon fresh lemon juice
¾	cup granulated sugar
2	tablespoons all-purpose flour
1	teaspoon ground cinnamon
¼	teaspoon ground nutmeg
⅛	teaspoon salt
2	tablespoons butter, cut into small pieces

Prep Time: 10 to 15 minutes
Baking Time: 50 to 60 minutes
Equipment: 9-inch pie pan, measuring spoons, measuring cups, rolling pin, rolling surface, large bowl, cooling rack

1. Preheat the oven to 425 degrees F. Take out a 9-inch pie pan.
2. Roll out the top and bottom pie crusts to 11-inch circles. Fit the bottom crust in the pie pan and trim the dough even with the rim of the pan. Refrigerate both the top and bottom crusts while making the filling.
3. Prepare the filling. In a large bowl, combine the apples and lemon juice.
4. Add the sugar, flour, cinnamon, nutmeg, and salt, and mix well.
5. Pile the apple mixture in the bottom pie crust, mounding it in the center so it rises an inch or so above the rim of the pan.
6. Distribute the butter on top of the apples.
7. Cover the filling with the top crust. Press the top and bottom crust edges together. Fold the top crust overhang underneath the bottom crust (as if you were tucking in a sheet). Make a raised ridge and flute or seal the edges. Cut 3 to 4 slits in the top crust.
8. Bake the pie for 10 minutes. Reduce the temperature to 350 degrees F and continue baking for 40 to 50 minutes, or until the top of the crust is golden and the filling is bubbling. Check the pie during the second half of baking to make sure

the crust is not overbrowning and the filling is not bubbling over. If necessary, shield the crust with foil and slip a foil-covered baking sheet under pie.

9. Cool the pie slightly on a rack before serving.

Yield: Serves 6 to 8

VARIATION

Dutch Apple Pie: *Make extra-large slits in the top crust. Pour ¹/₂ cup heavy cream through the slits 5 minutes before the end of the baking time. Serve warm.*

French Apple Pie: *Replace the top crust with streusel: Mix 1 cup flour, ¹/₂ cup cold butter, and ¹/₂ cup brown sugar until crumbly. Omit step 6.*

Latticed Top: *Apples look beautiful peeking out from beneath a latticed top crust.*

Extra-Fruity Pie: *Mix 1 cup cranberries or ¹/₂ cup raisins into the apple mixture, or substitute 2 cups of pears for apples.*

Cheddar's Better: *Top the apples with thin slices of sharp cheddar before adding the crust, or serve with a wedge of cheddar cheese.*

Apple Pie à la Mode: *Top the warm pie with vanilla or cinnamon ice cream.*

TIPS

Fresh fruit tastes much better than canned fruit. Try to use fruit in season at the peak of its flavor.

Use fresh, firm, flavorful, tart apples for pie. Excellent apples to use include Granny Smith, Golden Delicious, Jonathan, Cortland, Rome, Baldwin, and Winesap.

One pound of apples equals three medium apples or three cups of sliced apples.

Use just enough sugar to enhance the fruit's flavor. Measurements can vary depending on the fruit's natural sweetness. Taste the mixture before adding the entire amount of sugar called for.

The acid in lemon juice retards discoloration and balances the natural fruit flavor.

Adjust the amounts of cinnamon and nutmeg to suit your taste.

If the apple mixture is excessively moist, use a slotted spoon to transfer the apples from the mixing bowl to the pie crust, or add an additional tablespoon of flour.

You can thicken the fruit mixture with cornstarch instead of flour. Use half as much cornstarch as flour.

For a nice finish, lightly glaze the top crust with an egg wash before baking.

To test for doneness, insert a knife through one of the vents to make sure the apples have softened. The apples should not stick to the tip of the knife.

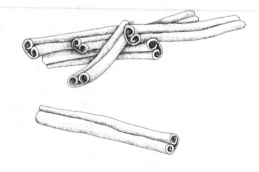

Peach Pie

Pastry for 9-inch double-crust pie (see recipe, page 160)

Filling

5	to 6 cups peaches, pitted, peeled, and sliced
1	tablespoon fresh lemon juice (optional)
¾	cup granulated sugar
¼	cup all-purpose flour
¼	teaspoon ground cinnamon (optional)
⅛	teaspoon ground nutmeg (optional)
2	tablespoons butter, cut into small pieces

This is a favorite that celebrates the abundant, sweet, and full-flavored peaches of summer.

Prep Time: 10 to 15 minutes
Baking Time: 40 to 50 minutes
Equipment: 9-inch pie pan, measuring spoons, measuring cups, rolling pin, rolling surface, large bowl, cooling rack

1. Preheat the oven to 425 degrees F. Take out a 9-inch pie pan.
2. Roll out the top and bottom pie crusts to 11-inch circles. Fit the bottom crust in the pie pan and trim the dough even with the rim of the pan. Refrigerate both the top and bottom crusts while making the filling.
3. Prepare the filling. In a large bowl, combine the peaches and lemon juice.
4. Add the sugar, flour, cinnamon, and nutmeg, and mix well.
5. Pile the peach mixture in the bottom pie crust and distribute the butter on top of the peaches.
6. Cover the filling with the top crust. Press the top and bottom crust edges together. Fold the top crust overhang underneath the bottom crust (as if you were tucking in a sheet). Make a raised ridge and flute or seal the edges. Cut 3 to 4 slits in the top crust.
7. Bake the pie for 10 minutes. Reduce the temperature to 350 degrees F and continue baking for 30 to 40 minutes, or until the top of the crust is golden and the filling is bubbling. Check the pie during the second half of baking to make sure the crust is not overbrowning and the filling is not bubbling

over. If necessary, shield the crust with foil and slip a foil-covered baking sheet under pie.

8. Cool the pie slightly on a rack before serving.

Yield: Serves 6 to 8

VARIATIONS

Latticed Top: *Peaches look beautiful peeking out from beneath a latticed top crust.*

Mixed Fruit Pie: *Substitute or mix fresh nectarines, plums, or apricots for some or all of the peaches.*

TIPS

Fresh fruit tastes much better than canned fruit. Try to use fruit in season at the peak of its flavor.

One pound of peaches equals four or five peaches or about two cups of sliced peaches.

Use firm, unbruised peaches for best results. Look for creamy yellow or gold background color. A red blush is a varietal characteristic and does not necessarily indicate ripeness.

To quickly ripen peaches, place them in a paper bag with an apple or banana (which give off ethylene gas), and store at room temperature out of direct sunlight.

To peel peaches easily, drop them in boiling water for fifteen seconds. Their skins will come right off.

Use just enough sugar to enhance the fruit's flavor. Measurements can vary depending on the fruit's natural sweetness. Taste the mixture before adding the entire amount called for.

The acid in lemon juice retards discoloration and balances the natural fruit flavor.

Adjust the amounts of cinnamon and nutmeg to suit your taste.

You can thicken the fruit mixture with cornstarch instead of flour. Use half as much cornstarch as flour.

For a nice finish, lightly glaze the top crust with an egg wash before baking.

Pumpkin Pie

~ ~

Pastry for 9-inch single-crust pie (see recipe, page 160)

Filling

2	eggs
2	cups (16 ounces) pumpkin, canned unsweetened or puréed fresh cooked
1 1/2	cups (12 ounces) evaporated milk
3/4	cup light brown sugar, firmly packed
2	teaspoons ground cinnamon
1	teaspoon ground ginger
1/2	teaspoon ground cloves
1/2	teaspoon ground nutmeg
1/2	teaspoon salt

This autumnal dessert really gives us something to be thankful for.

Prep Time: 10 to 15 minutes
Baking Time: 55 to 65 minutes
Equipment: 9-inch pie pan, measuring spoons, measuring cups, rolling pin, rolling surface, large bowl, cooling rack

1. Preheat the oven to 425 degrees F. Take out a 9-inch pie pan.
2. Roll out the crust to an 11-inch circle. Fit it in the pie pan and trim a 3/4-inch overhang. Fold the overhang under itself (like making a hem) until even with the rim of the pan. For a plain edge, press the dough flat; for a fluted edge, pinch up the dough to make a raised ridge, and flute. Refrigerate while making the filling.
3. Prepare the filling. In a large bowl, beat the eggs.
4. Add the pumpkin, evaporated milk, sugar, cinnamon, ginger, cloves, nutmeg, and salt. Mix well.
5. Pour the filling into the pie crust.
6. Bake for 15 minutes. Reduce the temperature to 350 degrees F and continue baking for 40 to 50 minutes, or until the crust is golden, the edges are set, and the center is almost set. Don't overbake. Check the pie during the second half of baking to make sure the crust is not overbrowning. If necessary, shield the crust with foil.
7. Cool the pie on a rack before serving.

Yield: Serves 6 to 8

The First Book of Baking

Maple Pumpkin Pie: *Substitute $^1/_2$ cup maple syrup for $^1/_2$ cup evaporated milk.*

Ginger Pecan Topping: *Mix $^1/_2$ cup brown sugar, $^1/_2$ cup coarsely chopped pecans, 2 tablespoons butter, and 2 tablespoons chopped crystallized ginger. Sprinkle on the baked pie after cooling. Broil for 1 to 2 minutes, or until bubbly.*

TIPS

Use brown sugar instead of granulated sugar to give the pie a slight molasses flavor.

You can substitute cream or milk for the evaporated milk.

If you use canned pumpkin, make sure to use solid-packed pumpkin, not pumpkin pie filling.

To eliminate the risk of spills when moving the pie from the counter to the oven, set the pie crust on the oven rack before filling. Transfer the filling to a pitcher to make pouring easier.

To prepare fresh pumpkin, cut one pound of peeled pumpkin meat into half-inch pieces. Steam the pumpkin for twenty-five minutes, stirring occasionally for even cooking. Cool to room temperature and purée.

Make your own pumpkin pie spice to keep on hand: Mix four teaspoons cinnamon, two teaspoons ginger, one teaspoon nutmeg, and one teaspoon cloves. Store tightly sealed in a cool place. Use two teaspoons per pie.

Remember, do not overbake the pie. Although the center (about the size of a quarter) may jiggle slightly when you gently shake the pan, the pie will become firm as it cools.

Another test for doneness is to insert a knife near the edge of the pie. If it comes out clean, the pie is done.

Store pumpkin pie in the refrigerator or freezer.

Strawberry-Rhubarb Pie

๛ ๙

Pastry for 9-inch double-crust pie (see recipe, page 160)

Filling

3	cups rhubarb, sliced into 1-inch pieces
2	cups strawberries, washed, hulled, and halved
1¼	cups granulated sugar
⅓	cup all-purpose flour
2	tablespoons butter, cut into small pieces

Rhubarb is such a popular pie filling it is known as the "pie plant." Strawberries add sweetness and flavor to the rhubarb's tartness.

Prep Time: 10 to 15 minutes
Baking Time: 40 to 50 minutes
Equipment: 9-inch pie pan, measuring spoons, measuring cups, rolling pin, rolling surface, large bowl, cooling rack

1. Preheat the oven to 425 degrees F. Take out a 9-inch pie pan.
2. Roll out the top and bottom pie crusts to 11-inch circles. Fit the bottom crust in the pie pan and trim the dough even with the rim of the pan. Refrigerate both the top and bottom crusts while making the filling.
3. Prepare the filling. In a large bowl, combine the rhubarb and strawberries.
4. Add the sugar and flour and mix well.
5. Pile the rhubarb and strawberry mixture in the bottom pie crust and distribute the butter on top of the filling.
6. Cover the filling with the top crust. Press the top and bottom crust edges together. Fold the top crust overhang underneath the bottom crust (as if you were tucking in a sheet). Make a raised ridge and flute or seal the edges. Cut 3 to 4 slits in the top crust.
7. Bake the pie for 10 minutes. Reduce the temperature to 350 degrees F and continue baking for 30 to 40 minutes, or until the top of the crust is golden and the filling is bubbling. Check the pie during the second half of baking to make sure the crust is not overbrowning and the filling is not bubbling

over. If necessary, shield the crust with foil and slip a foil-covered baking sheet under the pie.

8. Cool the pie slightly on a rack before serving.

Yield: Serves 6 to 8

VARIATIONS

Latticed Top: *This ruby filling looks beautiful peeking out from beneath a latticed top crust.*

A Hint of Orange: *For a complementary citrus flavor, add the grated zest of 1 medium orange to the filling.*

TIPS

Fresh fruit tastes much better than canned fruit. Try to use fruit in season at the peak of its flavor.

Be careful when using rhubarb. Only the stalks are edible; its leaves contain oxalic acid and are poisonous.

Look for bright red or pink stalks of rhubarb. They should be firm and crisp. Avoid stalks that are very thick or wilted. To preserve crispness, wrap raw rhubarb tightly in plastic wrap and refrigerate for up to one week.

One pound of raw rhubarb yields two cups of sliced fruit.

If fresh rhubarb is not available, use frozen rhubarb.

Rhubarb can give off a lot of water when cooking. If strawberries are particularly juicy, add an extra tablespoon of flour to filling.

Use just enough sugar to enhance the fruit's flavor. Measurements can vary depending on the fruit's natural sweetness. Taste the mixture before adding the entire amount called for.

Adjust the spices to your liking. One teaspoon of cinnamon or nutmeg can enhance the pie's flavor.

You can thicken the fruit mixture with cornstarch instead of flour. Use half as much cornstarch as flour.

For a nice finish, lightly glaze the top crust with an egg wash before baking.

Blueberry Pie

Pastry for 9-inch double-crust pie (see recipe, page 160)

Filling

4   cups blueberries, washed and dried
1   tablespoon fresh lemon juice (optional)
¾   cup granulated sugar
¼   cup all-purpose flour
½   teaspoon ground cinnamon (optional)
2   tablespoons butter, cut into small pieces

Bake this summertime favorite when blueberries are growing wild and being sold at roadside stands.

Prep Time: 10 to 15 minutes
Baking Time: 40 to 50 minutes
Equipment: 9-inch pie pan, measuring spoons, measuring cups, rolling pin, rolling surface, large bowl, cooling rack

1. Preheat the oven to 425 degrees F. Take out a 9-inch pie pan.
2. Roll out the top and bottom pie crusts to 11-inch circles. Fit the bottom crust in the pie pan and trim the dough even with the rim of the pan. Refrigerate both the top and bottom crusts while making the filling.
3. Prepare the filling. In a large bowl, combine the blueberries and lemon juice.
4. Add the sugar, flour, and cinnamon, and mix well.
5. Pile the blueberry mixture in the bottom pie crust and distribute the butter on top of the berries.
6. Cover the filling with the top crust. Press the top and bottom crust edges together. Fold the top crust overhang underneath the bottom crust (as if you were tucking in a sheet). Make a raised ridge and flute or seal the edges. Cut 3 to 4 slits in the top crust.
7. Bake the pie for 10 minutes. Reduce the temperature to 350 degrees F and continue baking for 30 to 40 minutes, or until the top of the crust is golden and the filling is bubbling. Check the pie during the second half of baking to make sure the crust is not overbrowning and the filling is not bubbling

over. If necessary, shield the crust with foil and slip a foil-covered baking sheet under pie.

8. Cool the pie slightly on a rack before serving.

Yield: Serves 6 to 8

VARIATIONS

Latticed Top: *Blueberries look beautiful peeking out from beneath a latticed top crust.*

Mixed Berry Pie: *Substitute or mix boysenberries, olallieberries, blackberries, or raspberries for some or all of the blueberries.*

July Fourth Pie: *To keep in the red, white, and blue spirit, mix blueberries and raspberries and top with vanilla ice cream.*

TIPS

Fresh fruit tastes much better than canned fruit. Try to use fruit in season at the peak of its flavor.

Do not thaw frozen berries. If the berries are covered in frost, add an extra tablespoon of flour.

Use just enough sugar to enhance the fruit's flavor. Measurements can vary depending on the fruit's natural sweetness. Taste the mixture before adding the entire amount called for.

The acid in lemon juice balances the natural fruit flavor.

You can thicken the fruit mixture with cornstarch instead of flour. Use half as much cornstarch as flour.

For a nice finish, lightly glaze the top crust with an egg wash before baking.

Chocolate Cream Pie

Pastry for 9-inch single-crust pie (see recipe, page 160)

Filling

1	cup granulated sugar
¼	cup cornstarch
¼	teaspoon salt
4	egg yolks
3	cups milk
4	ounces unsweetened chocolate, chopped into small pieces
2	tablespoons butter
1	teaspoon vanilla extract

Whipped Cream

1	cup heavy cream
2	tablespoons confectioners' sugar
½	teaspoon vanilla extract

Is there any better comfort food than rich and creamy chocolate custard wrapped in flaky pastry and topped with whipped cream and chocolate shavings? Not likely.

Prep Time: 35 to 45 minutes, plus 3 hours to chill
Baking Time: 14 to 21 minutes
Equipment: 9-inch pie pan, measuring spoons, measuring cups, rolling pin, rolling surface, fork, cooling rack, heavy-bottomed medium-sized saucepan, whisk, medium bowl, large bowl, electric mixer

1. Preheat the oven to 425 degrees F. Take out a 9-inch pie pan.
2. Roll out the crust to an 11-inch circle. Fit it in the pie pan and trim a ¾-inch overhang. Fold the overhang under itself (like making a hem) until even with the rim of the pan. For a plain edge, press the dough flat; for a fluted edge, pinch up the dough to make a raised ridge, and flute. Prick the pastry shell at ½-inch intervals with a fork to prevent the dough from bubbling up. Refrigerate the crust for 30 minutes.
3. Line the pie pan with lightly greased aluminum foil, shiny side down. Weigh down the crust.
4. Bake the crust for 6 to 8 minutes. Reduce the temperature to 350 degrees F. Remove the foil and weights and bake for an additional 8 to 13 minutes, or until the crust is crisp and golden.
5. Cool the crust completely on a rack.

6. Meanwhile, prepare the filling. In a medium saucepan (off the heat), whisk the sugar, cornstarch, and salt. Set aside.

7. In a medium bowl, beat the egg yolks and milk together. Add them to the saucepan and whisk until the cornstarch dissolves.

8. Add the chopped chocolate.

9. Set the saucepan over medium heat, stirring frequently at first, then constantly as the mixture starts to thicken and simmer, about 8 to 10 minutes. Once the mixture reaches a boil (you'll see big bubbles bursting on the surface), stir constantly for 10 to 15 seconds.

10. Remove the saucepan from the heat and stir in the butter and vanilla until the butter melts.

11. Transfer the filling to a medium bowl. Press a piece of plastic wrap against the surface of the filling to prevent a skin from forming. Cool until warm, about 30 minutes.

12. Pour the warm filling into the pie crust. Place a piece of plastic wrap directly on the filling. Refrigerate the pie until completely chilled, at least 3 hours.

13. Just before serving, prepare the whipped cream. In a large bowl, with an electric mixer on medium-high speed, whip the cream to soft peaks. Add the sugar and vanilla and beat until stiff peaks form. Do not overbeat. Spread the whipped cream on the filling. Refrigerate until 30 minutes before serving.

Yield: Serves 6 to 8

(Continues)

Meringue Topping: *Top the pie with meringue (see recipe, page 177) while the filling is warm, and bake at 350 degrees F for 15 minutes. Cool completely before refrigerating.*

You're the Tops: *Top the pie with grated chocolate, chocolate shavings, or chocolate sprinkles.*

Tips

Unlike the fillings for fruit pies, which are usually baked in their crust, cream pie fillings are cooked first and then poured, partially set, into a prebaked pie crust or crumb crust.

Bake the crust a day ahead for quicker prep time the day of serving.

You can substitute a chocolate cookie crust for a pastry crust.

Check the crust during blind-baking to see if bubbles are forming. Prick the bubbles to deflate them.

To prevent scorching, cook the filling in a heavy saucepan, a double boiler, or a bowl placed over a saucepan of simmering water. Make sure to stir the perimeter of the pan as well as the center.

For a smoother filling, mix the dry ingredients thoroughly so the liquid will blend in easily.

Don't be alarmed if the filling seems thin. It will thicken as it cools and sets.

Store the pie in the refrigerator.

Lemon Meringue Pie

❧ ❧

Pastry for 9-inch single-crust pie (see recipe, page 160)

Filling
1¼ cups granulated sugar
6 tablespoons cornstarch
¼ teaspoon salt
1½ cups water
3 egg yolks
2 tablespoons butter
½ cup fresh lemon juice
1 tablespoon lemon zest, finely grated

Meringue
3 to 5 egg whites, room temperature
¼ teaspoon cream of tartar
6 tablespoons sugar

This is the roadside diner classic, piled high with luscious lemon filling and topped with clouds of airy meringue.

Prep Time: 35 to 45 minutes, plus 3 hours to set
Baking Time: 24 to 36 minutes, total
Equipment: 9-inch pie pan, measuring spoons, measuring cups, grater, rolling pin, rolling surface, fork, cooling rack, heavy-bottomed medium-sized saucepan, whisk, small bowl, large bowl, electric mixer, spoon

1. Preheat the oven to 425 degrees F. Take out a 9-inch pie pan.
2. Roll out the pie crust to an 11-inch circle. Fit it in the pie pan and trim a ¾-inch overhang. Fold the overhang under itself (like making a hem) until even with the rim of the pan. For a plain edge, press the dough flat; for a fluted edge, pinch up the dough to make a raised ridge, and flute. Prick the pastry shell at ½-inch intervals with a fork to prevent the dough from bubbling up. Refrigerate the crust for 30 minutes.
3. Line the pie pan with lightly greased aluminum foil, shiny side down. Weigh down the crust.
4. Bake the crust for 6 to 8 minutes. Reduce the temperature to 350 degrees F. Remove the foil and weights and bake for an additional 8 to 13 minutes, or until the crust is crisp and golden.
5. Cool the crust completely on a rack.
6. Meanwhile, prepare the filling. In a medium saucepan, whisk the sugar, cornstarch, and salt. Over medium-high heat, gradually stir in the water. Whisk for several minutes until smooth, thickened, bubbly, and translucent.

(Continues)

7. Reduce the heat to low and cook for 5 more minutes, stirring frequently, until the mixture looks clear and thick. Remove from the heat and set aside.
8. In a small bowl, beat the egg yolks.
9. Add about $\frac{1}{2}$ cup of the heated cornstarch mixture to the egg yolks, whisking vigorously. Pour the warmed yolk mixture back into the saucepan and blend.
10. Cook the mixture over medium heat, about 3 to 5 minutes stirring constantly. Remove from the heat. Add the butter, lemon juice, and lemon zest. Whisk well and set aside.
11. Preheat the oven to 350 degrees F.
12. Prepare the meringue. In a large bowl, beat the egg whites with an electric mixer on low speed until foamy (1 to $1\frac{1}{2}$ minutes). Stop the mixer and sprinkle the cream of tartar on top of the egg whites. Resume mixing, increasing the speed to medium, and beat until soft droopy peaks form when the beaters are withdrawn. The mixture will look like whipped marshmallow topping. This can take several minutes.
13. Reduce the speed to medium-low and add the sugar, 2 tablespoons at a time (make sure there are no lumps in the sugar before adding), beating after each addition. Keep beating until whites hold peaks that slightly droop at the top. The peaks should still be moist, perfectly smooth, and glossy looking. This can take several minutes.
14. Pour the warm filling into the prepared crust. Immediately spread the meringue over the filling, making sure to seal it around the edge of the crust. With the back of a spoon, shape the meringue into peaks and swirls.
15. Bake for 10 to 15 minutes, or until the meringue is lightly browned. Watch for burning.
16. Cool the pie on a rack for at least 3 hours before serving.

Yield: Serves 6 to 8

Mile-High Meringue: *Extra egg whites will add height to the meringue. For a mile-high pie, increase the cream of tartar to $1/2$ teaspoon and use 8 to 12 egg whites.*

TIPS

Bake the crust a day ahead for quicker prep time the day of serving.

Read "Beating and Folding Egg Whites," page 103, before starting the recipe.

One medium lemon yields almost one-quarter cup of juice and about one tablespoon of grated zest.

Always grate the lemon zest before squeezing the lemon for juice.

Grate only the yellow portion of the lemon peel. The white portion, known as the pith, is very bitter.

To get more juice from a lemon, microwave it on high for ten seconds or put it in a bowl of hot water for thirty minutes. Then roll it on the counter, pressing lightly, before squeezing the juice. This breaks up the membrane inside the lemon so that the juices will release more easily when squeezed.

To prevent scorching, cook the filling in a heavy saucepan, a double boiler, or in a bowl placed over a saucepan of simmering water. Make sure to stir the perimeter of the pan as well as the center.

Use a nonaluminum saucepan to prevent discoloration.

Some of the cornstarch mixture is quickly beaten into the egg yolks to warm them so they don't turn into scrambled eggs when mixed with the hot filling.

For a stiffer meringue, more suitable for piping, use four tablespoons of sugar for each egg white.

Spread the meringue over the still-warm filling. The heat will cook the underside of the meringue and prevent liquid forming between the meringue and the filling (known as "weeping").

To prevent the meringue from shrinking, spread it all the way to the edges so it adheres to the pie crust.

Avoid making meringue on a humid day. It will absorb the moisture from the air and become soggy.

Cool the pie away from drafty areas to prevent the meringue from pulling away from the crust.

If the meringue has become watery, remove the first slice of pie, tip the pan over the sink, and pour off any excess liquid.

Store the pie in the refrigerator.

Banana Cream Pie

Pastry for 9-inch single-crust pie (see recipe, page 160)

Filling
- ¾ cup granulated sugar
- ¼ cup cornstarch
- ¼ teaspoon salt
- 4 egg yolks
- 3 cups milk
- 2 tablespoons butter
- 2 teaspoons vanilla extract
- 2 large bananas, sliced

Whipped Cream
- 1 cup heavy cream
- 2 tablespoons confectioners' sugar
- ½ teaspoon vanilla extract

This creamy pie pairs satiny custard with slices of banana and tops it all off with a mound of whipped cream. It's another childhood favorite that will never go out of style.

Prep Time: 35 to 45 minutes, plus 3 hours to chill
Baking Time: 14 to 21 minutes
Equipment: 9-inch pie pan, measuring spoons, measuring cups, rolling pin, rolling surface, fork, cooling rack, heavy-bottomed medium-sized saucepan, whisk, medium bowl, large bowl, electric mixer

1. Preheat the oven to 425 degrees F. Take out a 9-inch pie pan.
2. Roll out the crust to an 11-inch circle. Fit it in the pie pan and trim a ¾-inch overhang. Fold the overhang under itself (like making a hem) until even with the rim of the pan. For a plain edge, press the dough flat; for a fluted edge, pinch up the dough to make a raised ridge, and flute. Prick the pastry shell at ½-inch intervals with a fork to prevent the dough from bubbling up. Refrigerate the crust for 30 minutes.
3. Line the pie pan with lightly greased aluminum foil, shiny side down. Weigh down the crust.
4. Bake the crust for 6 to 8 minutes. Reduce the temperature to 350 degrees F. Remove the foil and weights and bake for an additional 8 to 13 minutes, or until the crust is crisp and golden.
5. Cool the crust completely on a rack.
6. Meanwhile, prepare the filling. In a medium saucepan (off the heat) whisk the sugar, cornstarch, and salt. Set aside.

(Continues)

7. In a medium bowl, beat the egg yolks and milk together. Add them to the saucepan and whisk until the cornstarch dissolves.

8. Set the saucepan over medium heat, stirring frequently at first, then constantly as the mixture starts to thicken and simmer, about 8 to 10 minutes. Once the mixture reaches a boil (you'll see big bubbles bursting on the surface), stir constantly for 10 to 15 seconds.

9. Remove the saucepan from the heat and stir in the butter and vanilla until the butter melts.

10. Transfer the filling to a medium bowl. Press a piece of plastic wrap against the surface of the filling to prevent a skin from forming. Cool until warm, about 30 minutes.

11. Pour half of the warm filling into the pie crust and top with the sliced bananas. Pour the rest of the filling over the bananas. Place a piece of plastic wrap directly on the filling. Refrigerate the pie until completely chilled, at least 3 hours.

12. Just before serving, prepare the whipped cream. In a large bowl, with an electric mixer on medium-high speed, whip the cream to soft peaks. Add the sugar and vanilla and beat until stiff peaks form. Do not overbeat. Spread the whipped cream on the filling. Refrigerate until 30 minutes before serving.

Yield: Serves 6 to 8

Variations

Vanilla Cream Pie: *Omit the bananas.*

Coconut Cream Pie: *Omit the bananas. Lightly toast 1¹/₄ cups shredded sweetened coconut in a 350-degree-F oven until golden, about 7 to 10 minutes, stirring frequently to prevent burning. Stir 1 cup coconut into the filling after the butter has melted (step 9). Sprinkle the remaining ¹/₄ cup coconut on top of the whipped cream just before serving.*

The First Book of Baking

Meringue Topping: *Top the pie with meringue (see recipe, page 177) while the filling is warm and bake at 350 degrees F for 15 minutes. Cool completely before refrigerating.*

TIPS

Unlike the fillings for fruit pies, which are usually baked in their crust, cream pie fillings are cooked first and then poured, partially set, into a prebaked pie crust or crumb crust.

Bake the crust a day ahead for quicker prep time the day of serving.

You can substitute a cookie crust for the pastry crust.

Check the crust during blind-baking to see if bubbles are forming. Prick the bubbles to deflate them.

To prevent scorching, cook the filling in a heavy saucepan, a double boiler, or in a bowl placed over a saucepan of simmering water. Make sure to stir the perimeter of the pan as well as the center.

Use a nonaluminum saucepan to prevent discoloration.

For a smoother filling, mix the dry ingredients thoroughly so the liquid will blend in easily.

A vanilla bean adds a richer vanilla flavor than extract. Add the vanilla bean with the egg yolks (step 7) and remove it (scraping out the seeds into the filling) before you whisk in the butter.

Don't be alarmed if the filling seems thin. It will thicken as it cools and sets.

Store the pie in the refrigerator.

Fruit Cobbler
❧ ❧

Fruit Filling

6	to 7 cups fruit or berries
2	tablespoons fresh lemon juice (optional)
2	tablespoons all-purpose flour
½	to ¾ cup granulated sugar
2	tablespoons butter, cut into small pieces

Biscuit Dough

1½	cups all-purpose flour
2	teaspoons baking powder
¼	teaspoon salt
2	tablespoons sugar
¼	cup (½ stick) butter, chilled and cut into small pieces
½	cup milk

Glaze (optional)

2	tablespoons butter, melted
1	to 2 tablespoons sugar

This versatile deep-dish dessert celebrates the season's finest fruits by pairing them with an easy-to-prepare biscuit-like topping. Be creative: Roll out the dough like a crust, shape it as dumplings, or roll it out and cut decoratively.

Prep Time: 10 to 15 minutes
Baking Time: 35 to 45 minutes
Equipment: 1½- to 2-quart baking dish, measuring spoons, measuring cups, food processor or large bowl, cooling rack (rolling pin, rolling surface, cookie cutters, pastry brush, optional)

1. Preheat the oven to 425 degrees F.
2. Prepare the filling. In a baking dish, mix the fruit with lemon juice, flour, and sugar. Dot with butter. Set aside.
3. Prepare the biscuit dough. In a food processor fitted with a metal chopping blade, add the flour, baking powder, salt, and sugar. Pulse to combine (about four pulses).
4. Add the butter and pulse until the mixture resembles coarse crumbs (about ten pulses).
5. Add the milk and pulse until just combined and evenly moistened (about four or five pulses). Do not allow the dough to form a ball.
6. Transfer the dough to a lightly floured surface. Knead for about 30 seconds, pushing the dough with the palms of your hands, to make the dough less sticky.
7. Pat or roll the dough to fit the baking pan. It should be no more than ½-inch thick. Leave a ½- to ¾-inch overhang.

8. Cover the filling with the crust. Pat the crust down around the fruit and tuck the overhang under itself or under the edge of the pan to seal. Make sure the crust is securely adhered to the pan.
9. Cut 3 or 4 slits in the top crust. If you want a glazed crust, brush with melted butter and sprinkle with sugar.
10. Bake for 35 to 45 minutes, or until the crust is golden and the filling is bubbling. Check during the second half of baking to make sure the crust is not overbrowning and that the filling is not bubbling over. If necessary, shield the crust with foil and slip a foil-covered baking sheet under the cobbler.
11. Cool the cobbler slightly on a rack. Serve warm.

Yield: Serves 6 to 8

VARIATIONS

Dumpling or Cut-Out Top: *For a dumpling topping, form the dough into 3-inch flat cakes and place them 2 inches apart on top of the fruit. For a decorative cut-out crust, roll the dough ¹/₂-inch thick and cut out shapes using cookie cutters. Place the dough on top of the fruit.*

July Fourth Cobbler: *Mix blueberries, strawberries, and raspberries, and cut the crust with star-shaped cutters. Top with heavy cream or vanilla ice cream.*

TIPS

Cobblers can be made in any decorative, ovenproof baking dish that is deep enough to accommodate the fruit.

Use a combination of fruits or berries for cobblers.

For the best flavor, choose fruit in season at the peak of its flavor. Use apples and pears in the fall and winter; try blueberries, strawberries, peaches, and cherries in the summer.

For a more stewed taste and softer texture, simmer the filling in a saucepan for ten minutes before baking.

Cobblers are especially good topped with heavy cream or ice cream.

Key Lime Pie

Graham cracker cookie crust (see recipe, page 162)

Filling

4 egg yolks
½ cup lime juice, freshly squeezed
14 ounces sweetened condensed milk
1 tablespoon lime zest, finely grated (plus ½ teaspoon extra for decorating)

Whipped Cream

1 cup heavy cream
2 tablespoons confectioners' sugar
½ teaspoon vanilla extract

This tropical treat is too good to savor only on vacation. If Key limes aren't available, substitute local limes.

Prep Time: 10 to 15 minutes, plus 4 to 6 hours to chill
Baking Time: 20 to 25 minutes, total
Equipment: 9-inch pie pan, measuring spoons, measuring cups, grater, cooling rack, large bowl, electric mixer

1. Preheat the oven to 350 degrees F. Take out a 9-inch pie pan.
2. Bake the graham cracker crust for 8 to 10 minutes. Cool completely on a rack.
3. Prepare the filling. In a large bowl, beat the egg yolks with an electric mixer on medium speed, until thick and lemon colored.
4. On low speed, add the condensed milk, lime juice, and lime zest. Beat just until thick and smooth. Do not overbeat.
5. Scrape the filling into the prepared crust and bake for 12 to 15 minutes. Cool completely on a rack. Refrigerate until firm, 4 to 6 hours.
6. Just before serving, prepare the whipped cream. In a large bowl, with an electric mixer on medium-high speed, whip the cream to soft peaks. Add the sugar and vanilla and beat until stiff peaks form. Do not overbeat.
7. Spread the whipped cream on the filling. Top with the reserved zest and serve.

Yield: Serves 6 to 8

The First Book of Baking

Pastry Crust: *Replace the graham cracker crust with a prebaked and cooled pie crust.*

Meringue Topping: *Top the pie with meringue (see recipe, page 177) and bake at 350 degrees F for 15 minutes.*

TIPS

Key limes are smaller, more yellow, and milder than the Persian limes found in most markets.

Three large limes produce about one-half cup of juice.

Many bakeries use green food coloring to make their Key lime pies appear more green. Do not be alarmed if your pie is more yellow than you expected.

Many recipes do not require baking the filling. However, because salmonella can be present in raw eggs, I recommend baking the filling as a food safety precaution.

Store the pie in the refrigerator until thirty minutes before serving.

For easier whipping, chill the bowl and the beaters before beating the cream.

Whip the cream only until firm peaks form, or you will end up with butter.

Whip the cream as close to the serving time as possible. It will deflate if left for a long time in the refrigerator.

Mud Pie

Chocolate cookie crust
(see recipe, page 162)

This ice cream treat is served in a chocolate cookie crust and topped with hot fudge and whipped cream. Perfect for a summer night.

Hot Fudge Sauce
1/2 cup heavy cream
2 tablespoons butter, cut in pieces
2 cups (12 ounces) semi-sweet chocolate chips
1 teaspoon vanilla extract

Ice Cream
1 quart coffee ice cream (or other flavor)

Whipped Cream
1 cup heavy cream
2 tablespoons confectioners' sugar
1/2 teaspoon vanilla extract

Prep Time: 20 to 30 minutes, plus 1 to 3 hours to freeze
Baking Time: 5 minutes
Equipment: 9-inch pie pan, measuring spoons, measuring cups, cooling rack, medium-sized saucepan or double boiler, large bowl, electric mixer

1. Preheat the oven to 350 degrees F. Take out a 9-inch pie pan.
2. Bake the chocolate cookie crust for 5 minutes. Cool completely on a rack.
3. Prepare the hot fudge. In a saucepan on low heat, warm the cream and butter until just simmering (little bubbles will form around the edges).
4. Add the chocolate chips and stir until dissolved.
5. Add the vanilla and stir until completely blended.
6. Remove the pan from the heat and cool the sauce completely.
7. Spoon 1/2 cup of fudge sauce on the crust. Freeze the crust for 30 minutes.
8. Soften the ice cream to spreading consistency. Fill the crust with the ice cream, mounding it up in the center.
9. Freeze the pie 1 to 2 hours, or until firm.
10. Spread the remaining fudge sauce over the top of the ice cream, covering it completely. Smooth the top. Freeze the pie for 30 minutes, or until ready to serve.
11. Just before serving, prepare the whipped cream. In a large bowl, with an electric mixer on medium-high speed, whip the cream to soft peaks. Add the sugar and vanilla, and beat until stiff peaks form. Do not overbeat.

12. Spread the whipped cream on top of the fudge or pipe it decoratively around the edges of the crust.
13. Let the pie soften 10 minutes for easier slicing.

Yield: Serves 6 to 8

VARIATIONS

Crust Crazy: *Replace the chocolate crust with another type of cookie crust.*

Lots of Flavors: *Layer the pie with two or three flavors of ice cream, separating the layers with crushed nuts.*

Rocky Road: *Mix chocolate ice cream with $1/2$ cup chocolate chips, $1/2$ cup mini-marshmallows, and $1/4$ cup sliced almonds.*

You're the Tops: *Top with grated chocolate, chocolate curls, toasted coconut, or chopped nuts.*

Crazy for Fudge: *Try a different flavor fudge. For mocha hot fudge, dissolve 1 tablespoon instant coffee into mixture. For chocolate mint, add $1/4$ teaspoon peppermint extract to the fudge. For peanut butter hot fudge, stir in $1/4$ cup peanut butter to the warm fudge. For a chocolate almond flavor, omit the vanilla and add $1/4$ teaspoon almond extract to the fudge.*

Flavored Whipped Cream: *For flavored whipped cream, add one of the following after adding the sugar: 1 teaspoon instant coffee, 2 tablespoons cocoa, $1/2$ teaspoon almond extract, $1/2$ teaspoon cinnamon, $1/2$ teaspoon ginger, 1 teaspoon grated lemon or orange zest, or $1/2$ teaspoon peppermint extract.*

TIPS

For easier whipping, chill the bowl and the beaters before beating the cream.

Whip the cream only until firm peaks form, or you will end up with butter.

Whip the cream as close to the serving time as possible. It will deflate if left for a long time in the refrigerator.

The cornstarch in confectioners' sugar helps to stabilize whipped cream.

Heavy cream will double in volume when whipped.

Refrigerate whipped cream if not using right away.

Cover the pie with plastic wrap and store it in the freezer.

Cherry Pie

❧ ❧

Pastry for 9-inch double-crust pie (see recipe, page 160)

Filling
4   cups cherries, pitted
1   cup granulated sugar
¼   cup all-purpose flour
2   tablespoons butter, cut into small pieces

Many people who "cannot tell a lie" claim cherry pie is their favorite dessert. After tasting this pie, you'll understand why.

Prep Time: 10 to 15 minutes
Baking Time: 40 to 50 minutes
Equipment: 9-inch pie pan, measuring spoons, measuring cups, rolling pin, rolling surface, large bowl, cooling rack

1. Preheat the oven to 425 degrees F. Take out a 9-inch pie pan.
2. Roll out the top and bottom pie crusts to 11-inch circles. Fit the bottom crust in the pie pan and trim the dough even with the rim of the pan. Refrigerate both the top and bottom crusts while making the filling.
3. Prepare the filling. In a large bowl, combine the cherries, sugar, and flour, and mix well.
4. Pile the cherry mixture in the bottom pie crust and distribute the butter on top of the cherries.
5. Cover the filling with the top crust. Press the top and bottom crust edges together. Fold the top crust overhang underneath the bottom crust (as if you were tucking in a sheet). Make a raised ridge and flute or seal the edges. Cut 3 to 4 slits in the top crust.
6. Bake the pie for 10 minutes. Reduce the temperature to 350 degrees F and continue baking for 30 to 40 minutes, or until the top of the crust is golden and the filling is bubbling. Check the pie during the second half of baking to make sure the crust is not overbrowning and the filling is not bubbling

over. If necessary, shield the crust with foil and slip a foil-covered baking sheet under pie.

7. Cool the pie slightly on a rack before serving.

Yield: Serves 6 to 8

VARIATIONS

Latticed Top: *Cherries look beautiful peeking out from beneath a latticed top crust.*

A Hint of Almonds: *A hint of almond extract can enhance the cherry flavor. Add 1 teaspoon almond extract to the cherry mixture, or sprinkle the crust with toasted ground almonds or almond slivers before baking.*

TIPS

Fresh fruit tastes much better than canned fruit. Try to use fruit in season at the peak of its flavor.

For the best pies, use tart or sour red cherries. If you're using sweet cherries, decrease the amount of sugar to one-half cup.

Use cherries that are firm, shiny, and dry. Sticky cherries are overripe.

Always rinse and dry the cherries well.

If fresh cherries are not available, use frozen or canned pitted tart cherries packed in water and drain before using.

Use just enough sugar to enhance the fruit's flavor. Measurements can vary depending on the fruit's natural sweetness. Taste the mixture before adding the entire amount called for.

You can thicken the fruit mixture with cornstarch instead of flour. Use half as much cornstarch as flour.

Many bakeries use red food coloring to make their cherry pies seem artificially bright. Do not be alarmed if your pie is paler than expected.

For a nice finish, lightly glaze the top crust with an egg wash before baking.

Fruit Crisp

Fruit Filling

5   to 6 cups fruit or berries
2   tablespoons fresh lemon juice (optional)
2   tablespoons all-purpose flour
½   cup granulated sugar

Topping

1   cup all-purpose flour
1   cup brown sugar, firmly packed
½   cup oats (optional)
2   teaspoons ground cinnamon
¼   teaspoon salt
½   cup (1 stick) butter, chilled, cut into pieces

Another winning way to celebrate the season's harvest is to team the freshest fruits with a crunchy crumb topping that's quick to prepare and is guaranteed to score praise every time it is served.

Prep Time: 10 to 15 minutes
Baking Time: 35 to 45 minutes
Equipment: 1½- to 2-quart baking dish, measuring spoons, measuring cups, food processor or large bowl, cooling rack

1. Preheat the oven to 375 degrees F.
2. Prepare the filling. In a baking dish, mix the fruit with lemon juice, flour, and sugar. Set aside.
3. Prepare the topping. In a food processor fitted with a metal chopping blade, add the flour, brown sugar, oats, cinnamon, and salt. Pulse to mix (about four pulses).
4. Add the butter and pulse until the mixture is moistened but crumbly (about five to ten pulses).
5. Sprinkle the topping over the fruit.
6. Bake for 35 to 45 minutes, or until the top is browned and crisp and the filling is bubbling. Check during the second half of baking to make sure the top is not overbrowning and that the filling is not bubbling over. If necessary, shield the top with foil and slip a foil-covered baking sheet under the crisp.
7. Cool the crisp slightly on a rack. Serve warm.

Yield: Serves 6 to 8

Going Crisp Crazy: *To vary the topping, add $^1/_3$ cup chopped or sliced nuts, 2 tablespoons crystallized ginger, or $^1/_4$ cup shredded coconut to the topping mixture.*

July Fourth Crisp: *Mix blueberries, strawberries, and raspberries. Top with heavy cream or vanilla ice cream.*

TIPS

Crisps can be made in any decorative, ovenproof baking dish that is deep enough to accommodate the fruit.

Use a combination of fruit or berries for crisps.

For the best flavor, choose fruit in season at the peak of its flavor. Use apples and pears in the fall and winter; try blueberries, strawberries, peaches, and cherries in the summer.

You can also use your fingertips to mix the crumb topping. If you do, use butter at room temperature.

Crisps are especially good topped with heavy cream or ice cream.

Pecan Pie

Pastry for 9-inch single-crust pie (see recipe, page 160)

Filling

3	eggs
1	cup light corn syrup
¾	cup light brown sugar, firmly packed
4	tablespoons (½ stick) butter, melted
1	teaspoon vanilla extract
¼	teaspoon salt
1½	cups pecans, chopped or whole

For many, Thanksgiving wouldn't seem complete without this rich and gooey treat.

Prep Time: 10 to 15 minutes
Baking Time: 45 to 55 minutes
Equipment: 9-inch pie pan, measuring spoons, measuring cups, rolling pin, rolling surface, large bowl, cooling rack

1. Preheat the oven to 350 degrees F. Take out a 9-inch pie pan.
2. Roll out the crust to an 11-inch circle. Fit it in the pie pan and trim a ¾-inch overhang. Fold the overhang under itself (like making a hem) until even with the rim of the pan. For a plain edge, press the dough flat; for a fluted edge, pinch up the dough to make a raised ridge, and flute. Refrigerate while making the filling.
3. Prepare the filling. In a large bowl, lightly beat the eggs.
4. Add the corn syrup, sugar, butter, vanilla, and salt, and mix until just blended.
5. Stir in the pecans and pour into the pie crust.
6. Bake for 45 to 55 minutes, or until the crust is golden, the edges are set, and the center is almost set (still jiggles slightly when lightly shaken). Don't overbake. Check the pie during the second half of baking to make sure the crust is not over-browning. If necessary, shield the crust with foil.
7. Cool the pie on a rack before serving.

Yield: serves 6 to 8

The First Book of Baking

Chocolate Pecan Pie: *Add 4 ounces melted chocolate to the filling.*

Mocha Pecan Pie: *Dissolve 3 tablespoons unsweetened cocoa and 2 teaspoons instant espresso or coffee powder into the melted butter before adding it to the filling.*

Spiked Pecan Pie: *Add 2 tablespoons rum or bourbon to the filling.*

Pecan Pie à la Mode: *Top the pie with vanilla ice cream.*

Extra-Nutty Pecan Pie: *Mix 1/2 cup chopped pecans into the filling and decoratively arrange 1 cup pecan halves in concentric circles on top of the pie before baking.*

TIPS

For a richer pecan flavor, toast the nuts in a 350-degree-F oven for six to eight minutes.

Use dark brown sugar and dark corn syrup for a pie with deeper color and a more caramel flavor.

If a foam forms on the filling during mixing, you are beating too vigorously. Skim it off before pouring it into the crust to prevent a mottled surface.

Sweet Potato Pie

Pastry for 9-inch single-crust pie (see recipe, page 160)

Filling

2	eggs
2	cups sweet potatoes, cooked, peeled, and mashed
4	tablespoons (½ stick) butter, melted
¾	cup brown sugar, firmly packed
1	cup milk
1	teaspoon ground cinnamon
½	teaspoon ground allspice
½	teaspoon ground nutmeg
¼	teaspoon salt

This Southern specialty is colorful and wonderfully aromatic. A truly American pie.

Prep Time: 10 to 15 minutes
Baking Time: 60 to 70 minutes
Equipment: 9-inch pie pan, measuring spoons, measuring cups, rolling pin, rolling surface, large bowl, spatula, cooling rack

1. Preheat the oven to 425 degrees F. Take out a 9-inch pie pan.
2. Roll out the crust to an 11-inch circle. Fit it in the pie pan and trim a ¾-inch overhang. Fold the overhang under itself (like making a hem) until even with the rim of the pan. For a plain edge, press the dough flat; for a fluted edge, pinch up the dough to make a raised ridge, and flute. Refrigerate while making the filling.
3. Prepare the filling. In a large bowl, beat the eggs.
4. Add the sweet potatoes, butter, brown sugar, milk, cinnamon, allspice, nutmeg, and salt. Mix well. The mixture will be thick.
5. Pour the filling into the pie crust. Smooth the top with a spatula.
6. Bake for 10 minutes. Reduce the temperature to 350 degrees F and continue baking for 50 to 60 minutes, or until the crust is golden, the edges are set, and the center is almost set. Don't overbake. Check the pie during the second half of baking to make sure the crust is not overbrowning. If necessary, shield the crust with foil.
7. Cool the pie on a rack before serving.

Yield: Serves 6 to 8

Pecan Sweet Potato Pie: *Add 3/4 cup chopped pecans to filling.*

Spiked Sweet Potato Pie: *Add 3 tablespoons bourbon or brandy to filling.*

Orange Sweet Potato Pie: *Add the juice of 1 medium orange and 1 tablespoon grated orange zest to the filling.*

TIPS

One to one-and-one-quarter pounds of sweet potatoes equals three to four medium potatoes or two cups of mashed potatoes.

Bake sweet potatoes at 450 degrees F for fifty to sixty minutes, or until very tender. Peel them and mash with a potato masher. Bake the sweet potatoes the day before to save prep time.

You can substitute cream, half-and-half, or evaporated milk for the milk for a richer-tasting pie.

Remember, do not overbake the pie. Although the center (about the size of a quarter) may jiggle slightly when you gently shake the pan, the pie will become firm as it cools.

Another test for doneness is to insert a knife near the edge of the pie. If it comes out clean, the pie is done.

Store sweet potato pie in the refrigerator.

BREADS

For many bakers, bread making is part baking, part therapy. Beginning so humbly as a mixture of flour, water, and yeast, bread dough becomes your personal punching bag as it is knocked around and kneaded. Given a little time to sit, it rises into a pillow of smooth and satiny dough. Removed from the oven, all crusty and warm, it's hard to resist the temptation to eat the entire loaf immediately.

Of all types of baking, bread making is one of the most forgiving. But be forewarned, it is also one of the most addicting. Once you've experienced the comforting and welcoming aroma of bread baking in your oven and have savored the incomparable taste of a warm loaf, baking your own bread will become a hard habit to break.

Equipment

BOWLS AND PANS

- Use a large bowl, preferably one with steeply sloping sides (to help the dough rise), for mixing and for holding the rising dough.

- Glass and ceramic bowls shorten the rising time because they hold the warmth of the dough better than metal bowls, but metal and plastic bowls are perfectly acceptable.
- Use medium-weight metal or clear glass pans to bake bread. A dark pan will produce a loaf with a thick, dark crust. You can use the most common-sized loaf pans—9 by 5 by 3 inches and 8½ by 4½ by 2½ inches—interchangeably. You can also use decorative clay or ceramic pans.
- Use dark, heavy-gauge aluminum baking sheets for baking free-form loaves, rolls, and baguettes. Baguette pans, with trough-shaped bottoms, help shape the loaves and produce more evenly cooked crusts. Some also have air holes that allow air to circulate from all sides, resulting in crisper crusts.

OTHER EQUIPMENT

- To ensure proper water temperature, use a thermometer that registers between 100 and 130 degrees F.
- Bread making is truly a "hands-on" activity: Use your hands or a sturdy spoon (heavy wooden spoons are particularly good) to mix ingredients before manually kneading the dough.
- A heavy-duty electric mixer equipped with a dough hook is helpful for mixing and kneading dough.
- You can also use a heavy-duty food processor to mix and knead dough. Make sure the work bowl can hold the necessary flour. A processor with a four-cup work bowl can handle about two cups of flour, a six-cup bowl can handle four cups of flour, and an eight-cup bowl can handle six cups of flour.
- A pastry or dough scraper is helpful for lifting and turning the dough during kneading. The blade should be thin and flexible. A four-inch putty knife is a good substitute.

The First Book of Baking

- Baking tiles or pizza stones help produce a thick-crusted free-form loaf. Place them in the oven before preheating.
- Cooling racks allow air to freely circulate on all sides of the bread.

Ingredients

FLOUR

- Bread flour, available at most supermarkets, has a higher protein count than all-purpose flour and contains bromate, an oxidizing agent, that strengthens the gluten and results in increased expansion and a chewier texture. If bread flour is unavailable, you can use either unbleached or bleached all-purpose flour, although unbleached flour has slightly more protein. Try to use flour that has at least twelve to thirteen grams of protein per cup.
- Whole wheat flour is milled from the entire wheat kernel (unlike all-purpose white flour, which is made only from the endosperm, the inner part of the wheat kernel). Because it contains the wheat's bran (full of fiber) and germ (rich in vitamins) in addition to the endosperm, whole wheat flour retains all the nutrients of the whole grain and does not need to be chemically enriched. Because it is not chemically treated, whole wheat flour is more perishable and should be stored in a cool place. Look for whole wheat flour that has been stone-ground rather than commercially ground for a higher vitamin content. Whole wheat flour is generally used in combination with white flour.

YEAST

- Yeast, a harmless sugar fungus, produces carbon dioxide gas bubbles that force the dough to expand and rise. When mixed with water it becomes rehydrated and begins to grow. As it feeds off of the sugar and flour in the dough, it rapidly multiplies.

- Dry yeast is available in individual packets (containing about two-and-one-half teaspoons) or in jars. Fresh yeast, also known as compressed yeast, is packaged as cakes and can be used interchangeably with dry yeast.
- If your package of yeast doesn't have an expiration date, test it before using: Mix one package of dry yeast, one teaspoon of sugar, and one-quarter cup of lukewarm water (between 105 and 110 degrees F) and leave it in a warm, dry spot for five minutes. If the mixture bubbles and froths, the yeast is viable and can be used in the recipe.
- Store dry yeast in a cool, dry place or in the refrigerator or freezer; it will stay fresh for about a year.
- Fresh yeast lasts two weeks in the refrigerator or up to two months in the freezer.

Water or Liquid

- Water is usually used to dissolve and activate yeast, but other liquids (milk, juice, yogurt) will also work.
- Yeast works best in a warm environment, so the liquid in the recipe should be between 105 and 110 degrees F. This temperature should feel comfortably warm, like a baby's bathwater. Water that is too hot will kill the yeast. Water that is too cold will not activate the yeast.
- Liquids also moisten the flour, beginning the gluten development. If your tap water is highly chlorinated or very hard, it is best to use springwater.

Other Ingredients

- Sugar or other sweeteners help the yeast grow and add flavor to the bread.
- Salt enhances the flavor of bread and inhibits the yeast's growth. This prevents the bread from overrising and collapsing. Do not mix salt directly with yeast during proofing.

The First Book of Baking

- Butter or oil add tenderness to bread.
- Cornmeal prevents dough from sticking to the baking surface. It acts like little ball bearings to create a platform for the dough to sit on, and allows the bread to be easily transferred to a baking stone.

Bakin' Bread

MIXING THE DOUGH

- There are two basic methods for using dry yeast in bread making. The most common method is to dissolve the yeast with warm liquid, often with a small amount of sugar added, before you combine it with the dry ingredients. This is known as "proofing" the yeast. The advantage of using this process is you can confirm the potency of the yeast before you proceed with the recipe.
- In the other proofing method, the yeast is mixed with the dry ingredients before the liquid is added. The liquid needs to be very warm (about 120 to 130 degrees F) because the dry ingredients cool the liquid before it makes contact with the yeast. The benefit of this one-step system is its convenience. Use this method only when you are sure the yeast is potent.
- When adding yeast to a liquid, whisk the yeast and liquid together and let stand several minutes to dissolve. Then whisk again to evenly disperse the yeast in the liquid before combining it with the dry ingredients.
- To make the dough, vigorously mix the dry ingredients with the yeast mixture and any other liquids, until the dough becomes stiff and begins to clean the sides of the bowl. The dough will be quite sticky and messy.
- Unlike other types of baking, the amount of flour used in bread making is imprecise. Different harvests, different

brands, different types of storage, and even the day's humidity will affect the flour's ability to absorb moisture. This makes it necessary for many recipes to give a range for the amount of flour needed. Use the minimum called for as a guide, and add the remaining flour, as needed, to achieve the desired consistency. On very humid days, you might need even more flour than the recipe calls for because the flour absorbs the moisture from the air. On dry days you'll need less flour. You can add flour during mixing (if the dough isn't pulling away from the bowl or becoming stiff) and during kneading (if it isn't forming a shiny and elastic mass). If you've added too much flour and the dough seems excessively stiff, add water, a tablespoon at a time, until the dough becomes soft and workable.

KNEADING THE DOUGH

- The height of your work surface is important when kneading. You should be able to comfortably rest the palms of your hand on the counter without feeling you are bending down or reaching up.
- Before kneading, dust your hands and the work surface with flour. Turn the dough out on the work surface, cleaning the bowl completely.
- Kneading is a rhythmic motion that incorporates the flour into the dough, completes the mixing process, and develops the dough's gluten. Gluten, which gives the bread its finished texture, is a strong, elastic network that holds the air bubbles that are created by the carbon dioxide that is released as the yeast feeds on the flour.
- To properly knead the dough by hand, first flatten it into a circle. Then, using the heel of your palms, bear down on the dough and push it away from you. Fold the dough partially back on itself and give it a quarter-turn. Repeat the pushing, folding, and turning again and again, adding a little more flour if the dough becomes too sticky. Kneading should take five to ten minutes.

- During kneading, add just enough flour so the dough is not too sticky to work with. Too much added flour may produce streaks, uneven grain, and densely textured bread.
- Knead the dough until it is shiny, smooth, and elastic, and it no longer sticks to the work surface.
- Here are three good ways to test if dough has been kneaded enough: Press the heel of your palm firmly into the dough for ten seconds (it should come away clean). Or, stretch a small piece of dough (it should be elastic and smooth, without any big holes). Or, poke the dough with your fingertips (it should spring back). With any of these methods, the dough should look like a cohesive mass that you can hold in your hand.
- You can use an electric mixer or food processor to both mix and knead, but finishing the kneading manually will help you to better judge the elasticity of the dough.

RAISING THE DOUGH

- After the kneading is complete, place the dough in a lightly greased bowl for its first rise. To prevent the surface from drying out and becoming hard, rotate the dough in the bowl, coating it completely. Cover the bowl with plastic wrap or a clean cloth and let it sit in a warm environment. The rising time will vary based on many variables, especially the strength of the yeast and the room temperature.
- The rise, also known as proofing, allows the yeast to ferment and provides time for the dough to develop its structure.
- Most breads use the two-rise method. One rise after the dough is kneaded, and another rise after the dough is shaped.
- Dough rises best in a warm, draft-free place between 75 and 85 degrees F. Place the dough in a sunny location or in an unheated oven with a pilot light. Do not put the dough over direct heat.
- It is better to put the dough in a place that is too cool rather than too hot. Excessive heat will force the dough to rise too

quickly, sacrificing the fermentation needed to develop the dough's flavor and texture. The slower the rise, the more flavorful the bread will be.

- You do not need to become a prisoner in your kitchen when making bread. If you need to slow down the rise, simply cover the dough with plastic wrap and refrigerate. This is helpful if you have to leave the rising dough for an extended period, or if you want to prepare the dough in advance. Dough can even be left overnight to rise in the refrigerator. Return the dough to room temperature to complete the rise.

- Dough should double in size during the first rise. To prevent overrising, make a mental note of how high the finished dough should be before you leave it.

- After the first rise, the dough should be swollen and puffy and will usually have a few blisters on top.

- To test if dough has properly risen, press two fingers into the dough near the edge, about one-half to one inch deep. If the dents remain, the dough is ready. If the dents fill in quickly, let it rise another fifteen minutes and test again.

- If well-kneaded dough hasn't risen at all after a couple of hours, the yeast has probably expired. To repair the dough, get some new yeast and dissolve the required amount in a little warm water. Spread out the dough and flatten it. Sprinkle the dissolved yeast, a little at a time, over the dough, and knead until the dough has absorbed all the fresh yeast. Add a little more flour to compensate for the liquid and knead to distribute the yeast thoroughly. Continue the recipe.

- Overrising the dough does not result in an extra-large loaf. Overrising exhausts the yeast and results in bread that lacks good flavor and texture.

The First Book of Baking

Shaping the Dough

- After the dough has risen, turn it out on a lightly floured surface. Deflate the dough and knead for one minute to work out all of the incorporated air and to return the dough to its original unleavened state.
- Shape the bread into its final form and place it in the baking pan or on the baking sheet for its last rise.
- If you're baking the dough in a loaf pan, the shaped dough should just barely touch the sides. The pan should be two-thirds full.
- If you're baking shaped loaves on a baking sheet, leave enough room for each loaf to expand threefold during the final rise and baking.
- If you're baking bread on a pizza stone or baking tiles, shape the dough on a cornmeal-coated sideless baking sheet.
- Bread can be shaped long and thin, like a baguette; oval, like an Italian bread; or rounded, like a country hearth bread.
- Cover the dough with plastic wrap or a clean cloth and place it in a warm spot to rise again.
- After the second rise, the dough should double in size and look puffy.
- Do not let the dough rise more than is directed or it could sink during baking. If the dough has risen to more than double its size, punch it down, knead for a minute or two, reshape it, and let it rise again.

The Crust

- For a nicely finished crust, apply a glaze before baking. For a dark finish, brush the dough with milk or an egg yolk mixed with a little water. For a slightly dark, shiny finish, mix a whole egg with a little water. For a clear shine, use an egg white and water mixture. If desired, add sesame or poppy seeds to the crust right after glazing.

- Cut shallow slashes with a razor or sharp knife to give a pattern to the finished loaf. Slashing the top of the bread also allows moisture to escape as the bread bakes.

BAKING

- Prepare the oven. Position the oven rack in the middle of the oven if using a baking sheet or baking pan. If baking in loaf pans, position the rack so the top of the pans will be level with, or slightly above, the middle of the oven.
- Always preheat the oven for at least fifteen minutes before the end of the last rise. You will have to approximate the time, as the length of the rise is variable.
- If baking on a pizza stone or baking tiles, place them on the bottom rack of the oven and preheat for thirty minutes. When heated, sprinkle the stone or tiles with cornmeal and transfer the bread from the baking sheet to the oven with a quick jerking motion.
- When baking two loaf pans at the same time, stagger them so there is at least one to two inches between the pans and the sides of the oven.
- If baking on a baking sheet, place it in the middle of the oven. Don't bake with two baking sheets in the oven at the same time. The air will not be able to circulate properly. If using two sheets, refrigerate one while the other bakes.
- When dough is placed in an oven, there is an immediate sudden rise before the yeast is killed by the heat. This is known as "oven spring."
- For a thick, crisp crust, it is necessary to create steam in the oven. You can achieve this effect in a home oven in three ways: Mist the loaves with water from a spray bottle; put a

pan of boiling water in the bottom of the oven during baking; or throw a handful of ice cubes onto the hot oven floor once or twice during baking.

- Cover the loaves with foil if they are browning too quickly during baking.
- The bread is done when the crust has browned, the loaves have shrunk away from the sides of the pan (if using a pan), and the loaf sounds hollow (a flat thud) when tapped on the bottom. If there is a question of doneness, insert a knife or toothpick in the bottom of the bread. It should come out free of dough.
- For a softer crust, brush the bread lightly with oil or melted butter after baking.
- Remove the bread from the pan immediately after baking to prevent the crust from becoming soggy. Let it cool on a rack so air can circulate all around it.

SLICING

- Let the bread cool completely before slicing.
- Slice the bread with a serrated knife, using a back-and-forth sawing motion.
- During slicing, if you find the bread is underdone, return it to a preheated oven for ten to fifteen minutes.

STORING

- Most bread tastes best the day it is baked.
- Store bread uncovered, at room temperature, the day it is baked. The bread's crust retains moisture and protects the loaf from becoming stale.
- To recrisp bread, place in a preheated 350-degree-F oven for five to eight minutes, or until the bread is thoroughly heated.

- If you're not using the bread the day it's baked, wrap it airtight and freeze. Breads can be frozen for up to six months. Label and date before freezing.
- Thaw bread in its wrapping for two to three hours or overnight at room temperature. To test if a loaf has thawed, stick a sharp knife into it for a few seconds. If the knife comes out cold, the bread needs more time.
- To reheat frozen bread, place it in a preheated 300-degree-F oven. For a crisp-crusted loaf, remove the wrapping, place it on a baking sheet, and heat for twenty to thirty minutes. For a soft-crusted loaf, unwrap it and brush away any ice crystals, then rewrap it in foil and heat for twenty to thirty minutes.

The First Book of Baking

White Bread

❧ ❧

2 cups warm water (about 110 degrees F)
1 package (2½ teaspoons) active dry yeast
5 to 6 cups flour (all-purpose, bread, or a combination)
1 tablespoon salt
2 tablespoons granulated sugar
2 tablespoons butter, melted and cooled to lukewarm
1 tablespoon oil or melted butter (for greasing the bowl)

This delicious white bread is shaped and baked in a loaf pan. After you taste it, it will be hard to eat store-bought sandwich bread again.

Prep Time: 25 to 35 minutes, plus 2 to 3 hours for rising
Baking Time: 25 to 35 minutes
Equipment: two 9 by 5 by 3-inch loaf pans, measuring spoons, measuring cups, large bowl, medium bowl, cooling rack (electric mixer or food processor, optional)

1. In a medium bowl, sprinkle the yeast over the warm water and let stand 3 to 5 minutes to dissolve.
2. In a large bowl, mix 5 cups of the flour with the salt and sugar.
3. Add the yeast mixture and butter, and stir vigorously until the dough becomes stiff and begins to clean the sides of the bowl. The dough will be quite sticky and messy.

    If you're using an electric mixer with a dough hook: Proceed with steps 1 through 3. Mix on low speed for 5 minutes, or until the dough is smooth and elastic. If the dough is excessively sticky, add the remaining flour, a tablespoon at a time. Advance to step 5.

    If you're using a food processor fitted with a metal chopping blade: Proceed with steps 1 through 3. Process until the dough forms a ball. If the dough is excessively sticky or will not form a ball, add flour, a tablespoon at a time. Advance to step 5.

(Continues)

4. Turn out the dough on a lightly floured surface. Flour your hands and knead the dough for 8 to 10 minutes, or until it is smooth, shiny, and elastic. If the dough is excessively sticky during kneading, add flour, a tablespoon at a time.
5. Transfer the dough to a lightly greased large bowl and rotate to coat all sides. Cover the bowl with plastic wrap or a clean cloth and leave the dough to double in size, 1 to 2 hours.
6. Lightly grease the loaf pans.
7. Turn the risen dough out on a lightly floured surface. Punch down and knead briefly to deflate the dough.
8. Divide the dough into 2 equal pieces. Shape each piece of dough into a 10 by 8-inch rectangle. Fold in the short sides until the dough is 1 to 2 inches smaller than the length of the pan, then fold the long ends into thirds, as if you are folding a letter into an envelope. Pat down to seal edges. Place the loaves in the pans, seam sides down. Cover with plastic wrap or a clean cloth. Allow to rise until doubled, about 1 hour.
9. Fifteen minutes before the end of the second rise, heat the oven to 400 degrees F.
10. When the loaves have risen, bake for 25 to 35 minutes, until golden brown and firm. Remove the bread from the pans and tap the bottoms of the loaves. They should sound hollow.
11. Cool the loaves completely on a rack.

Yield: 2 loaves

The First Book of Baking

Cinnamon Raisin Swirl: *Combine 1 tablespoon cinnamon and 3 table-spoons sugar with 2 tablespoons softened butter. In step 8, shape each piece of dough into a rectangle and spread half of the mixture over the surface of the dough. Press 1/3 cup raisins on top of the cinnamon mixture. Proceed with folding and shaping.*

TIPS

Melt the butter just until most of it liquefies. Stir until all of the butter dissolves.

Substitute warm milk for water for a creamier taste, softer crumb, and darker crust. The bread will stay softer longer.

To test if the dough has been kneaded enough, press the heel of your palm firmly into the dough for ten seconds (it should come away clean), stretch a small piece of dough (it should be elastic and smooth), or poke the dough with your fingertips (it should spring back).

To test if the dough has properly risen, press two fingers into the dough, one-half inch deep. If the dents remain, the dough is ready. If the dents fill in quickly, let rise another fifteen minutes before testing again.

If only one bread pan is available, place the shaped dough in the refrigerator while baking the first loaf.

Sourdough Bread
❧ ❧

Starter
2 cups warm water (about 110 degrees F)
1 package (2½ teaspoons) active dry yeast
2 cups flour (all-purpose, bread, or a combination)
1 tablespoon sugar

Sponge
1¼ cups warm water (about 110 degrees F)
1 cup starter
2 cups flour (all-purpose, bread, or a combination)
1 teaspoon sugar

Dough
Sponge
3 to 4 cups flour
2 teaspoons salt
1 tablespoon melted butter or oil (for greasing the bowl)
1 to 2 tablespoons cornmeal (for sprinkling the baking sheet)

Making sourdough bread is a multiday activity. First a flour and water "starter" is left out for days to ferment and sour naturally. The starter is then mixed with more flour and water to create a "sponge" and left overnight to develop. The following day the mixing, kneading, and rising take place. This lengthy development creates the unique sourdough taste and texture.

Prep Time: 35 to 45 minutes, plus 2 to 3½ hours for rising
Baking Time: 30 to 40 minutes
Equipment: baking sheet, measuring spoons, measuring cups, medium bowl, large bowl, knife, cooling rack (electric mixer or food processor, optional)

1. Prepare the starter. In a medium bowl, sprinkle the yeast over the warm water. Stir to dissolve. Add the flour and sugar, and stir until smooth. Cover the bowl with cheesecloth and let it stand in a warm place for 5 to 10 days, stirring 2 or 3 times a day, until the mixture has a sour and fermented aroma. The starter might bubble or have a yellow liquid layer on top. Stir well before using, or refrigerate for later use (bring the starter back to room temperature before using).

2. When the starter is ready, make the sponge. In a large bowl, combine the water, starter, flour, and sugar until smooth. Leave uncovered to ferment overnight in a warm place. The mixture will sour and bubble.

3. Prepare the bread. Stir the sponge to remove its crust and deflate. Add 3 cups of the flour and the salt. Stir vigorously until the dough begins to clean the sides of the bowl. The dough will be stiff but soft.

If you're using an electric mixer with a dough hook: Proceed with steps 1 through 3. Mix on low speed for 5 to 10 minutes, or until the dough is smooth and elastic. If the dough is excessively sticky, add the remaining flour, a tablespoon at a time. Advance to step 5.

If you're using a food processor fitted with a metal chopping blade: Proceed with steps 1 through 3. Process until the dough forms a ball. If the dough is excessively sticky or will not form a ball, add flour, a tablespoon at a time. Advance to step 5.

4. Turn out the dough on a lightly floured surface. Flour your hands and knead the dough for 8 to 10 minutes, or until it is smooth, shiny, and elastic. If the dough is excessively sticky during kneading, add flour, a tablespoon at a time.

5. Transfer the dough to a lightly greased large bowl and rotate to coat all sides. Cover the bowl with plastic wrap or a clean cloth and leave the dough to double in size, 1 to 2 hours.

6. Turn the risen dough out onto a lightly floured surface. Punch down and knead briefly to deflate the dough.

7. Divide the dough into 2 equal pieces. Shape each piece of dough into a 15 by 10-inch rectangle. Roll up the dough lengthwise, jelly-roll fashion. Pinch the ends and edges together to seal. With both hands starting in the center of the loaf, rock gently back and forth, moving each hand away from the center to lengthen the loaf and taper the ends.

8. Sprinkle the baking sheet with cornmeal. Place the loaves on the baking sheet. Let rise, uncovered, until doubled in size, 1 to 1½ hours.

9. Fifteen minutes before the end of the second rise, heat the oven to 400 degrees F.

(Continues)

10. When the loaves have risen, use a sharp knife to make ¼-inch-deep diagonal slashes in the dough at 2-inch intervals. Bake for 30 to 40 minutes, or until golden brown and firm. Remove the bread from the sheet and tap the bottoms of the loaves. They should sound hollow.
11. Cool the loaves completely on a rack.

Yield: 2 long loaves or 2 round loaves

TIPS

The easiest way to make a sourdough starter is to borrow or buy some existing starter from another source (a friend, store, or mail-order) and add flour and water to increase its volume.

There are many different starter recipes. Essentially, all that matters is that the yeast ferments and goes sour. Some starters depend entirely on wild yeast to ferment the mixture. However, because the amount of natural yeast in everyone's home varies greatly, this recipe calls for the addition of a small amount of yeast to "jump-start" the starter.

Do not use rapid-rise yeast when making the starter.

Fermentation time depends on many factors, especially the weather; the warmer the temperature, the faster the starter will develop. If the starter is left out to sour for more than one week, add a teaspoon of sugar to feed the yeast.

Once the starter is ready, use or refrigerate.

Use or replenish the refrigerated starter at least once a week. To replenish starter, add equal amounts of lukewarm water and flour (usually one cup of each), stir, cover with a clean cloth, and leave out overnight. The starter will become bubbly and rise. Stir, cover, and refrigerate in the morning. If you don't use it every week, stir in one teaspoon of sugar or honey to keep the starter active. A well-fed starter will last indefinitely in the refrigerator.

Bring refrigerated starter to room temperature before using, preferably overnight.

The First Book of Baking

If your starter turns pink or orange, it may contain bacteria. Throw it out and thoroughly wash your container in hot water.

If mold grows on the starter, throw it out and start again.

Use glass, ceramic, or wooden utensils to store and stir your starter. Prolonged contact with metal can alter its character and flavor.

Do not store the starter in a container with a tight-fitting lid. Some gaseous expansion can occur and put pressure on the seal. Use a crock jar with a nonscrew lid, or cover loosely.

The longer the starter is kept and replenished, the more authentic the taste of each successive loaf.

Starters can be frozen for six months. Let frozen starter stand twenty-four hours at room temperature for it to become active again.

Sourdough bread tends to absorb a lot of flour during kneading. Keep the work space and your hands lightly floured, and add flour very gradually, if needed.

To test if the dough has been kneaded enough, press the heel of your palm firmly into the dough for ten seconds (it should come away clean), stretch a small piece of dough (it should be elastic and smooth), or poke the dough with your fingertips (it should spring back).

To test if the dough has properly risen, press two fingers into the dough, one-half inch deep. If the dents remain, the dough is ready. If the dents fill in quickly, let rise another fifteen minutes before testing again.

Bread can also be shaped into rounded loaves and baked in round cake pans that have been sprinkled with cornmeal.

Coating the baking sheet with cornmeal prevents the bread from sticking.

Baking directly on a preheated pizza stone or baking tiles will make the bottom crust extra crispy. Place the stone or tiles in the oven before preheating. Before transferring the bread to the oven, coat the stone or tiles with cornmeal. With a quick jerking motion, transfer the bread from a sideless baking sheet to the oven. The cornmeal on the baking sheet will act like little ball bearings and allow the dough to slide right off.

For a darker crust, glaze with egg wash before baking.

Whole Wheat Bread

2	cups warm water (about 110 degrees F)
1	package (2½ teaspoons) active dry yeast
2	cups whole wheat flour
3	to 3½ cups flour (all-purpose, bread, or a combination)
1	tablespoon salt
¼	cup granulated sugar
4	tablespoons (½ stick) butter, melted and cooled to lukewarm
1	tablespoon oil or melted butter (for greasing the bowl)

This hearty wheat loaf contains the nutrients and fiber of the entire wheat kernel. It's great for sandwiches or toast.

Prep Time: 25 to 35 minutes, plus 2 to 3 hours for rising
Baking Time: 25 to 35 minutes
Equipment: two 9 by 5 by 3-inch loaf pans, measuring spoons, measuring cups, large bowl, medium bowl, cooling rack (electric mixer or food processor, optional)

1. In a medium bowl, sprinkle the yeast over the warm water and let stand 3 to 5 minutes to dissolve.
2. In a large bowl, mix the whole wheat flour and 3 cups of the white flour with the salt and sugar.
3. Add the yeast mixture and butter, and stir vigorously until the dough becomes stiff and begins to clean the sides of the bowl. The dough will be quite sticky and messy.

    If you're using an electric mixer with a dough hook: Proceed with steps 1 through 3. Mix on low speed for 5 minutes, or until the dough is smooth and elastic. If the dough is excessively sticky, add the remaining flour, a tablespoon at a time. Advance to step 5.

    If you're using a food processor fitted with a metal chopping blade: Proceed with steps 1 through 3. Process until the dough forms a ball. If the dough is excessively sticky or will not form a ball, add flour, a tablespoon at a time. Advance to step 5.

The First Book of Baking

4. Turn out the dough on a lightly floured surface. Flour your hands and knead the dough for 8 to 10 minutes, or until it is smooth, shiny, and elastic. If the dough is excessively sticky during kneading, add white flour, a tablespoon at a time.

5. Transfer the dough to a lightly greased large bowl and rotate to coat all sides. Cover the bowl with plastic wrap or a clean cloth and leave the dough to double in size, 1 to 2 hours.

6. Lightly grease the loaf pans.

7. Turn the risen dough out on a lightly floured surface. Punch down and knead briefly to deflate the dough.

8. Divide the dough into 2 equal pieces. Shape each piece of dough into a 10 by 8-inch rectangle. Fold in the short sides until the dough is 1 to 2 inches smaller than the length of the pan, then fold the long ends into thirds, as if you are folding a letter into an envelope. Pat down to seal edges. Place the loaves in the pans, seam sides down. Cover with plastic wrap or a clean cloth. Allow to rise until doubled, about 1 hour.

9. Fifteen minutes before the end of the second rise, heat the oven to 400 degrees F.

10. When the loaves have risen, bake for 25 to 35 minutes until brown and firm. Remove the bread from the pans and tap the bottoms of the loaves. They should sound hollow.

11. Cool the loaves completely on a rack.

Yield: 2 loaves

VARIATIONS

Honey–Whole Wheat Bread: *Substitute honey for sugar. Add honey in step 3.*

Seedy Whole Wheat Bread: *Add 1/4 cup sunflower seeds, 2 tablespoons poppy seeds, and 3 tablespoons toasted sesame seeds (step 2).*

Melt the butter just until most of it liquefies. Stir until all of the butter dissolves.

Substitute warm milk for water for a creamier taste, softer crumb, and darker crust. The bread will stay softer longer.

To test if the dough has been kneaded enough, press the heel of your palm firmly into the dough for ten seconds (it should come away clean), stretch a small piece of dough (it should be elastic and smooth), or poke the dough with your fingertips (it should spring back).

To test if the dough has properly risen, press two fingers into the dough, one-half inch deep. If the dents remain, the dough is ready. If the dents fill in quickly, let rise another fifteen minutes before testing again.

If only one bread pan is available, place the shaped dough in the refrigerator while baking the first loaf.

Dinner Rolls

¾ cup milk
¼ cup water
¼ cup (½ stick) butter
3 to 3½ cups flour (all-purpose, bread, or a combination)
1 package (2½ teaspoons) active dry yeast
3 tablespoons sugar
1 teaspoon salt
1 egg, lightly beaten
1 tablespoon butter, melted (for greasing the bowl)

Shape these versatile rolls simply for every day, or more decoratively for entertaining.

Prep Time: 30 to 40 minutes, plus 1 to 2 hours for rising
Baking Time: 15 to 20 minutes
Equipment: baking sheet, measuring spoons, measuring cups, medium saucepan, large bowl, cooling rack (electric mixer or food processor, optional)

1. In a saucepan over low heat, stir the milk, water, and butter until very warm and the butter almost melts (120 to 130 degrees F). Remove from the heat and stir until the butter dissolves.
2. In a large bowl, mix 3 cups of the flour with the yeast, sugar, and salt.
3. Blend the milk mixture into the dry ingredients.
4. Add the egg.

    If you're using an electric mixer with a dough hook: Proceed with steps 1 through 4. Mix on low speed for 30 seconds then on high speed for 3 minutes, or until the dough is smooth and elastic. If the dough is excessively sticky, add the remaining flour, a tablespoon at a time. Advance to step 7.

    If you're using a food processor fitted with a metal chopping blade: Proceed with steps 1 through 4. Process until the dough forms a ball. If the dough is excessively sticky or will not form a ball, add flour, a tablespoon at a time. Advance to step 7.

5. Stir vigorously until the dough cleans the sides of the bowl. The dough will be soft and moist.

(Continues)

6. Turn out the dough on a lightly floured surface. Flour your hands and knead the dough for 5 to 8 minutes, or until it is smooth, shiny, and elastic. If the dough is excessively sticky during kneading, add flour, a tablespoon at a time.

7. Transfer the dough to a lightly buttered large bowl and rotate to coat all sides. Cover the bowl with plastic wrap or a clean cloth and leave the dough to double in size, 45 to 60 minutes.

8. Just before end of first rise, lightly grease a baking sheet.

9. Turn the risen dough out on a lightly floured surface. Punch down and knead briefly to deflate the dough.

10. Divide the dough into 12 equal pieces. Shape each piece into a ball, pulling the edges underneath to make a smooth top. Place the balls smooth side up on the baking sheet, leaving 2 to 3 inches between rolls.

11. Cover with plastic wrap or a clean cloth. Allow to rise until doubled, 25 to 45 minutes.

12. Fifteen minutes before the end of the second rise, heat the oven to 400 degrees F.

13. When the rolls have risen, bake for 15 to 20 minutes, or until they are golden brown and firm.

14. Remove the rolls from the baking sheet to a cooling rack.

Yield: 12 rolls

VARIATIONS

Cloverleaf Rolls: *Lightly grease a muffin tin. Divide the dough into 12 equal pieces. Divide these into 3 equal pieces, and shape each piece into a small ball. Place 3 balls in each muffin cup to make a cloverleaf shape. Let rise until doubled, about 25 to 45 minutes. Bake 15 to 20 minutes, or until golden brown.*

Crescent Rolls: *Lightly grease a baking sheet. On a lightly floured surface, roll out the dough into a 12-inch circle. Cut the dough into 8 triangles, as if cutting a pizza. Lightly brush each triangle with melted butter. Beginning at the wide end of the triangle, roll toward the point. Place the rolls on a baking sheet, tip-side down, and curve the ends to make a crescent shape. Let rise until doubled, about 25 to 45 minutes. Bake 15 to 20 minutes, or until golden brown.*

Seeds on Top: *Before baking, glaze the rolls with an egg wash and sprinkle on sesame seeds or poppy seeds.*

TIPS

The yeast is not proofed first, so use yeast that you know is potent.

To test if the dough has been kneaded enough, press the heel of your palm firmly into the dough for ten seconds (it should come away clean), stretch a small piece of dough (it should be elastic and smooth), or poke the dough with your fingertips (it should spring back).

To test if the dough has properly risen, press two fingers into the dough, one-half inch deep. If the dents remain, the dough is ready. If the dents fill in quickly, let rise another fifteen minutes before testing again.

You can make these rolls a day ahead. Simply refrigerate the dough after step 7. When you're ready to bake, remove the rolls from the refrigerator, shape, and let rise until doubled, 35 to 50 minutes. Bake as directed.

After baking, brush the tops with melted butter for a softer crust. Glaze rolls with egg wash before baking for a shiny, thicker crust.

French Bread

❧ ❧

These crusty long loaves, known as baguettes, have soft, chewy centers. To develop the texture and flavor of authentic French bread, a third rising is recommended.

1⅓ cups warm water (about 110 degrees F)

1 package (2½ teaspoons) active dry yeast

3 to 3½ cups flour (all-purpose, bread, or combination)

2 teaspoons salt

1 tablespoon melted butter or oil (for greasing the bowl)

1 to 2 tablespoons cornmeal (for sprinkling the baking sheet)

2 cups boiling water (optional)

Prep Time: 30 to 40 minutes, plus 3 to 5 hours for rising
Baking Time: 25 to 35 minutes
Equipment: baking sheet, measuring spoons, measuring cups, medium bowl, large bowl, knife, small baking pan, cooling rack (electric mixer or food processor, optional)

1. In a medium bowl, sprinkle the yeast over the warm water and let stand 3 to 5 minutes to dissolve.
2. In a large bowl, mix 3 cups of the flour with the salt.
3. Add the yeast mixture and stir vigorously until the dough becomes stiff and begins to clean the sides of the bowl. The dough will be stiff but soft.

   If you're using an electric mixer with a dough hook: Proceed with steps 1 through 3. Mix on low speed for 5 minutes, or until the dough is smooth and elastic. If the dough is excessively sticky, add the remaining flour, a tablespoon at a time. Advance to step 5.

   If you're using a food processor fitted with a metal chopping blade: Proceed with steps 1 through 3. Process until the dough forms a ball. If the dough is excessively sticky or will not form a ball, add flour, a tablespoon at a time. Advance to step 5.

4. Turn out the dough on a lightly floured surface. Flour your hands and knead the dough for 8 to 10 minutes, or until it is smooth, shiny, and elastic. If the dough is excessively sticky during kneading, add flour a tablespoon at a time.

5. Transfer the dough to a lightly greased large bowl and rotate to coat all sides. Cover the bowl with plastic wrap or a clean cloth and leave the dough to double in size, 1 to 2 hours.

6. Turn the risen dough out on a lightly floured surface. Punch down and knead briefly to deflate the dough. Return to the bowl and let the dough rise again until doubled in size, 1 to 2 hours.

7. Again, turn the risen dough out on a lightly floured surface. Punch down and knead briefly to deflate the dough.

8. Divide the dough into 2 equal pieces. Shape each piece of dough into a 15 by 10-inch rectangle. Roll up the dough lengthwise, jelly-roll fashion. Pinch the ends and edges together to seal. With both hands starting in the center of the loaf, rock gently back and forth, moving each hand away from the center to lengthen the loaf and taper the ends.

9. Sprinkle the baking sheet with cornmeal. Place the loaves on the baking sheet. Let rise, uncovered, until doubled in size, about 1 hour.

10. Fifteen minutes before the end of the third rising, heat the oven to 450 degrees F. Prepare the boiling water.

11. When the loaves have risen, brush them with cold water. With a sharp knife, make 1/4-inch-deep diagonal slashes in the dough at 2-inch intervals. Pour boiling water in a small baking pan on the floor of the oven to create steam. Bake for 25 to 35 minutes, or until golden brown and firm. Remove the bread from the sheet and tap the bottoms of the loaves. They should sound hollow.

12. Cool the loaves completely on a rack.

Yield: 2 long loaves

(Continues)

Crusty Dinner Rolls: *Divide the dough into 15 equal pieces after the second rise. Shape into balls and let rise, uncovered, on lightly buttered baking sheet. Brush with water and bake 15 to 20 minutes.*

TIPS

To test if the dough has been kneaded enough, press the heel of your palm firmly into the dough for ten seconds (it should come away clean), stretch a small piece of dough (it should be elastic and smooth), or poke the dough with your fingertips (it should spring back).

To test if the dough has properly risen, press two fingers into the dough, one-half inch deep. If the dents remain, the dough is ready. If the dents fill in quickly, let rise another fifteen minutes before testing again.

Placing a pan of boiling water in the oven creates the steam needed to produce the thick crust typical of French bread. Spraying the bread with a misting bottle when it first goes in the oven and then again every two minutes for the first eight minutes also produces a thicker crust.

Baking directly on a preheated pizza stone or baking tiles will make the bottom crust extra crispy. Place the stone or tiles in the oven before preheating. Before transferring the bread to the oven, coat the stone or tiles with cornmeal. With a quick jerking motion, transfer the bread from a sideless baking sheet to the oven. The cornmeal on the baking sheet will act like little ball bearings and allow the dough to slide right off.

For a darker crust, glaze with egg wash before baking.

Focaccia

~~ ~~

Focaccia

1   cup warm water (about 110 degrees F)

1   package (2½ teaspoons) active dry yeast

3   to 3¼ cups flour (all-purpose, bread, or a combination)

2   teaspoons salt

¼   cup olive oil, plus extra for greasing the bowl and pan

Topping

1   tablespoon olive oil

1   to 2 teaspoons coarse salt

This Italian flatbread can be topped as simply or as elaborately as you desire. Bake unadorned and use for sandwiches, or cover with fancy toppings for an impressive appetizer.

Prep Time: 25 to 35 minutes, plus 1½ to 2 hours for rising
Baking Time: 25 to 30 minutes
Equipment: baking sheet, measuring spoons, measuring cups, large bowl (electric mixer or food processor, optional)

1. In a large bowl, sprinkle the yeast over the warm water and let stand 10 minutes to dissolve.

2. Add 3 cups of the flour with the salt and olive oil, and stir vigorously until the dough becomes stiff and begins to hold its shape. The dough will be sticky.

   If you're using an electric mixer with a dough hook: Proceed with steps 1 and 2. Mix on low speed for 2 minutes, or until the dough is smooth and elastic. If the dough is excessively sticky, add the remaining flour, a tablespoon at a time. Advance to step 4.

   If you're using a food processor: Proceed with steps 1 and 2. Process until the dough forms a ball. If the dough is excessively sticky or will not form a ball, add the flour, a tablespoon at a time. Advance to step 4.

3. Turn out the dough on a lightly floured surface. Flour your hands and knead the dough for 3 to 5 minutes, or until it is smooth, shiny, and elastic. If the dough is excessively sticky during kneading, add flour, a tablespoon at a time.

4. Transfer the dough to a lightly oiled large bowl and rotate to coat all sides. Cover the bowl with plastic wrap or a clean cloth and leave it to double in size, 45 to 60 minutes.

(Continues)

5. Lightly grease a baking sheet with olive oil.

6. Turn the risen dough out on a lightly floured surface. Punch down and knead briefly to deflate the dough.

7. Pat and press the dough to fit the baking pan. The dough should be between $\frac{1}{4}$ and $\frac{1}{2}$ inch thick. If the dough resists stretching, let it rest for a few minutes before continuing.

8. Cover the dough with plastic wrap or a clean cloth. Allow to rise until doubled, about 1 hour.

9. Fifteen minutes before the end of the second rise, heat the oven to 400 degrees F.

10. When the focaccia has risen, use your fingertips to poke deep indentations in the dough at 2-inch intervals. Brush with the remaining tablespoon of olive oil and sprinkle with coarse salt.

11. Bake for 25 to 30 minutes, or until golden and firm.

12. Cut into squares and serve immediately.

Yield: 6 to 8 servings

VARIATIONS

Focaccia Sandwiches: *Cut focaccia into squares and slice horizontally, or just add toppings for open-faced sandwiches.*

Crunchy Crust: *Add $\frac{1}{4}$ cup cornmeal to the dough (step 2).*

You're the Tops: *Before baking, sprinkle the dough with one or more of the following toppings: coarsely ground pepper, rosemary or other fresh herbs, grated Parmesan cheese, pine nuts, sun-dried tomatoes, golden raisins, herbes de Provence, garlic, sautéed onions, or olives.*

You can easily mix focaccia in a food processor because it uses less flour than other breads.

To test if the dough has been kneaded enough, press the heel of your palm firmly into the dough for ten seconds (it should come away clean), stretch a small piece of dough (it should be elastic and smooth), or poke the dough with your fingertips (it should spring back).

To test if the dough has properly risen, press two fingers into the dough, one-half inch deep. If the dents remain, the dough is ready. If the dents fill in quickly, let rise another fifteen minutes before testing again.

For even cooking, make sure the dough is an even thickness in the pan.

Check halfway through baking to make sure the bottom is not over-browning. If necessary, slide another baking pan underneath to insulate the bottom.

Baking focaccia directly on a preheated pizza stone or baking tiles will make the bottom crust extra crispy. Place the stone or tiles in the oven before preheating. Before transferring the focaccia to the oven, coat the stone or tiles with cornmeal.

Focaccia freezes well if wrapped airtight. To defrost, unwrap and reheat at 375 degrees F for about 5 to 10 minutes.

Pecan Sticky Rolls

~ ~

Dough

¾ cup milk
¼ cup (½ stick) butter
¼ cup granulated sugar
½ teaspoon salt
2½ to 3 cups flour (all-
  purpose, bread, or
  a combination)
1 package (2½ teaspoons)
  active dry yeast
2 eggs, lightly beaten
1 tablespoon butter,
  melted (for greasing
  the bowl)

Topping

5 tablespoons butter
⅔ cup brown sugar, firmly
  packed
2 tablespoons light corn
  syrup
1 cup pecans, coarsely
  chopped

Filling

¼ cup (½ stick) butter,
  softened
¼ cup brown sugar, firmly
  packed
1 tablespoon ground
  cinnamon

These gooey caramel rolls are a pecan lover's delight.

Prep Time: 30 to 40 minutes, plus 1½ to 2 hours for rising
Baking Time: 20 to 25 minutes
Equipment: 13 by 9 by 2-inch baking pan, measuring spoons, measuring cups, medium saucepan, large bowl, small bowl (electric mixer or food processor, optional)

1. Prepare the dough. In a saucepan over low heat, stir the milk, butter, sugar, and salt until very warm and the butter almost melts (120 to 130 degrees F). Remove from the heat and stir until the butter dissolves.

2. In a large bowl, mix 2½ cups of the flour with the yeast.

3. Blend the milk mixture into the dry ingredients.

4. Add the eggs.

   If you're using an electric mixer with a dough hook: Proceed with steps 1 through 4. Mix on low speed for 30 seconds, then on high speed for 3 minutes, or until the dough is smooth and elastic. If the dough is excessively sticky, add the remaining flour, a tablespoon at a time. Advance to step 7.

   If you're using a food processor fitted with a metal chopping blade: Proceed with steps 1 through 4. Process until the dough forms a ball. If the dough is excessively sticky or will not form a ball, add the flour, a tablespoon at a time. Advance to step 7.

5. Stir vigorously until the dough cleans the sides of the bowl. The dough will be soft and moist.

The First Book of Baking

6. Turn out the dough on a lightly floured surface. Flour your hands and knead the dough for 3 to 5 minutes, or until it is smooth, shiny, and elastic. If the dough is excessively sticky during kneading, add flour, a tablespoon at a time.

7. Transfer the dough to a lightly buttered large bowl and rotate to coat all sides. Cover the bowl with plastic wrap or a clean cloth and leave the dough to double in size, about 1 hour.

8. Just before the end of the first rise, take out a baking pan.

9. Prepare the topping. In a saucepan, combine the butter, brown sugar, and corn syrup over low heat until blended. Pour the mixture into the baking pan and sprinkle pecans evenly over the top. Set aside.

10. Prepare the filling. In a small bowl, mix the butter, brown sugar, and cinnamon to make a paste. Set aside.

11. Turn the risen dough out on a lightly floured surface. Punch down and knead briefly to deflate the dough. Shape the dough into a 14 by 8-inch rectangle. Spread the filling over the dough, leaving a 1/2-inch border around the edges.

12. Roll up the dough lengthwise, jelly-roll fashion. Pinch the edges and ends to seal. Cut the roll into 12 equal pieces. Arrange the rolls in the pan, cut side up, leaving 2 to 3 inches between rolls.

13. Cover with plastic wrap or a clean cloth. Allow to rise until doubled, 30 to 60 minutes.

14. Fifteen minutes before the end of the second rise, heat the oven to 375 degrees F.

15. When the rolls have risen, bake for 20 to 25 minutes, or until they are golden brown and firm.

16. Cool the rolls in the pan for 5 minutes. Invert the pan onto a plate and serve.

Yield: 12 rolls

(Continues)

Extra-Nutty Rolls: *Sprinkle $^1/_2$ cup chopped pecans or other nuts over the filling.*

TIPS

The yeast is not proofed first, so use yeast that you know is potent.

To test if the dough has been kneaded enough, press the heel of your palm firmly into the dough for ten seconds (it should come away clean), stretch a small piece of dough (it should be elastic and smooth), or poke the dough with your fingertips (it should spring back).

To test if the dough has properly risen, press two fingers into the dough, one-half inch deep. If the dents remain, the dough is ready. If the dents fill in quickly, let rise another fifteen minutes before testing again.

If you don't have a 13 by 9 by 2-inch baking pan, use another pan that fits the rolls with room to spare. The rolls will expand during the second rise, and then again while baking. If the rolls are placed too close together, their growth will be inhibited and they will take longer to bake.

When rolling up the dough, don't roll too tightly or it will not have space to rise fully.

For giant rolls: Roll up widthwise instead of lengthwise.

To easily cut rolls: Wrap dental floss or thick thread around the roll and pull tightly.

To prepare rolls for the next morning: Form the rolls. Before the second rise, place lightly greased waxed paper or plastic wrap directly on the rolls, and refrigerate. Before baking, let the rolls stand covered for twenty to thirty minutes at room temperature. Uncover (puncture any surface bubbles with a greased toothpick) and bake as directed above.

Cinnamon Rolls

Dough

¾ cup milk
¼ cup (½ stick) butter
¼ cup granulated sugar
½ teaspoon salt
2½ to 3 cups flour (all-purpose, bread, or a combination)
1 package (2½ teaspoons) active dry yeast
2 eggs, lightly beaten
1 tablespoon butter, melted (for greasing the bowl)

Filling

¼ cup (½ stick) butter, softened
¼ cup brown sugar, firmly packed
1 tablespoon ground cinnamon

Glaze

1 cup confectioners' sugar
1 tablespoon milk
½ teaspoon vanilla extract

These delicious cinnamon-swirled rolls are a breakfast treat. They're best right out of the oven, so prepare them a day ahead and bake the next morning.

Prep Time: 30 to 40 minutes, plus 1½ to 2 hours for rising
Baking Time: 20 to 25 minutes
Equipment: 13 by 9 by 2-inch baking pan, measuring spoons, measuring cups, medium saucepan, large bowl, small bowl, cooling rack (electric mixer or food processor, optional)

1. Prepare the dough. In a saucepan over low heat, stir the milk, butter, sugar, and salt until very warm and the butter almost melts (120 to 130 degrees F). Remove from the heat and stir until the butter dissolves.
2. In a large bowl, mix 2½ cups of the flour and the yeast.
3. Blend the milk mixture into the dry ingredients.
4. Add the eggs.

    If you're using an electric mixer with a dough hook: Proceed with steps 1 through 4. Mix on low speed for 30 seconds, then on high speed for 3 minutes, or until the dough is smooth and elastic. If the dough is excessively sticky, add the remaining flour, a tablespoon at a time. Advance to step 7.

    If you're using a food processor fitted with a metal chopping blade: Proceed with steps 1 through 4. Process until the dough forms a ball. If the dough is excessively sticky or will not form a ball, add flour, a tablespoon at a time. Advance to step 7.

5. Stir vigorously until the dough cleans the sides of the bowl. The dough will be soft and moist.

(Continues)

6. Turn out the dough on a lightly floured surface. Flour your hands and knead the dough for 3 to 5 minutes, or until it is smooth, shiny, and elastic. If the dough is excessively sticky during kneading, add flour, a tablespoon at a time.

7. Transfer the dough to a lightly buttered large bowl and rotate to coat all sides. Cover the bowl with plastic wrap or a clean cloth and leave the dough to double in size, about 1 hour.

8. Prepare the filling. In a small bowl, mix the butter, brown sugar, and cinnamon to make a paste. Set aside.

9. Just before the end of the first rise, lightly grease a baking pan.

10. Turn the risen dough out on a lightly floured surface. Punch down and knead briefly to deflate the dough. Shape the dough into a 14 by 8-inch rectangle. Spread the filling over the dough, leaving a 1/2-inch border around the edges.

11. Roll up the dough lengthwise, jelly-roll fashion. Pinch the edges and ends to seal. Cut the roll into 12 equal pieces. Arrange the rolls in the pan, cut side up, leaving 2 to 3 inches between rolls.

12. Cover with plastic wrap or a clean cloth. Allow to rise until doubled, 30 to 60 minutes.

13. Fifteen minutes before the end of the second rise, heat the oven to 375 degrees F.

14. When the rolls have risen, bake for 20 to 25 minutes, or until they are golden brown and firm.

15. Meanwhile, prepare the glaze. In a small bowl, mix the confectioners' sugar, milk, and vanilla until smooth.

16. Remove the rolls from the pan to a cooling rack. Glaze and serve warm.

Yield: 12 rolls

The First Book of Baking

Cinnamon Raisin Rolls: *Sprinkle $^1\!/_2$ cup raisins over the filling. If the raisins are very dry, plump them briefly in hot water.*

Cinnamon Nut Rolls: *Sprinkle $^1\!/_2$ cup chopped nuts over the filling.*

TIPS

The yeast is not proofed first, so use yeast that you know is potent.

To test if the dough has been kneaded enough, press the heel of your palm firmly into the dough for ten seconds (it should come away clean), stretch a small piece of dough (it should be elastic and smooth), or poke the dough with your fingertips (it should spring back).

To test if the dough has properly risen, press two fingers into the dough, one-half inch deep. If the dents remain, the dough is ready. If the dents fill in quickly, let rise another fifteen minutes before testing again.

If you don't have a 13 by 9 by 2-inch baking pan, use another pan that fits the rolls with room to spare. The rolls will expand during the second rise and then again while baking. If the rolls are placed too close to-gether, their growth will be inhibited and the insides will take longer to bake.

When rolling up the dough, don't roll too tightly or it will not have room to rise fully.

For giant rolls: Roll up widthwise instead of lengthwise.

To easily cut rolls: Wrap dental floss or thick thread around the roll and pull tightly.

To prepare rolls for the next morning: Form the rolls. Before the second rise, place lightly greased waxed paper or plastic wrap directly on the rolls and refrigerate. Before baking, let the rolls stand covered for twenty to thirty minutes at room temperature. Uncover (puncture any surface bubbles with a greased toothpick) and bake as directed above.

Pizza Dough

ᏝᏝ ᎧᎧ

1 cup warm water (about 110 degrees F)
1 package (2½ teaspoons) active dry yeast
3 cups flour (all-purpose, bread, or combination)
1 teaspoon salt
2 tablespoons olive oil, plus extra for greasing the bowl
1 to 2 tablespoons cornmeal (optional, for sprinkling)

This versatile dough tastes great with all kinds of sauces and toppings. For a really tasty pizza, try cooking it on the grill.

Prep Time: 25 to 35 minutes, plus 1 to 1½ hour for rising
Baking Time: 15 to 20 minutes
Equipment: baking sheet(s) or pizza pan(s), measuring spoons, measuring cups, large bowl, (electric mixer or food processor, optional)

1. In a large bowl, sprinkle the yeast over the warm water and let stand 10 minutes to dissolve.
2. Add the flour, salt, and olive oil, and stir vigorously until the dough becomes stiff and begins to hold its shape. The dough will be sticky.
    If you're using an electric mixer with a dough hook: Proceed with steps 1 and 2. Mix on low speed for 2 minutes, or until the dough is smooth and elastic. Advance to step 4.
    If you're using a food processor: Proceed with steps 1 and 2. Process until the dough forms a ball. Advance to step 4.
3. Turn out the dough on a lightly floured surface. Flour your hands and knead the dough for 3 to 5 minutes, or until it is smooth, shiny, and elastic.
4. Transfer the dough to a lightly oiled large bowl and rotate to coat all sides. Cover the bowl with plastic wrap or a clean cloth and leave the dough to double in size, about 1 hour.
5. When the dough has risen, heat the oven to 450 degrees F. Lightly coat a baking sheet or pizza pan with cornmeal.
6. Turn the risen dough out on a lightly floured surface. Punch down and knead briefly to deflate the dough. Let the dough rest 15 minutes.

7. Roll or stretch the dough to the desired size on a lightly floured surface. Transfer it to the baking sheet or pizza pan. Top with sauce and cheese.
8. Bake for 15 to 20 minutes, until the edges and bottoms are browned and the cheese has melted.
9. Serve immediately.

Yield: 1 large or 2 medium-sized pizzas

VARIATIONS

Whole Wheat Crust: *Substitute 1 cup whole wheat flour for 1 cup white flour.*

Herbed Crust: *Mix in 1 tablespoon fresh herbs (rosemary or oregano go well) (step 2).*

A Touch of Honey: *Add 1 tablespoon honey for a slightly sweet crust (step 2).*

Crunchy Crust: *Add 1/4 cup cornmeal to the crust (step 2).*

TIPS

Do not add extra flour. This will make the pizza dough tough.

You can easily mix pizza dough in a food processor because it uses less flour than other breads.

To test if the dough has been kneaded enough, press the heel of your palm firmly into the dough for ten seconds (it should come away clean), stretch a small piece of dough (it should be elastic and smooth), or poke the dough with your fingertips (it should spring back).

To test if the dough has properly risen, press two fingers into the dough, one-half inch deep. If the dents remain, the dough is ready. If the dents fill in quickly, let rise another fifteen minutes before testing again.

Baking pizza directly on a preheated pizza stone or baking tiles will make the bottom crust extra crispy. Place the stone or tiles in the oven before preheating. Before transferring the pizza to the oven, coat the stone or tiles with cornmeal.

Pizza can be cooked directly on the grill, but baking the pizza for 10 minutes before grilling firms up the dough and makes it easier to handle.

Index

A

Angel food cake
    basic, 126–128
    chocolate, 128
Apple pie
    basic, 163–165
    cranberry, 164
    Dutch, 164
    French, 164
    raisin, 164

B

Baking powder, about,
    4–5
Baking soda, about, 4–5
Banana
    bread, 40–41
    cream pie, 181–183
    nut muffins, 24–25
Biscotti
    basic, 79–81
    chocolate, 55–57
    chocolate chip, 80
    chocolate–chocolate
        chip, 56
    chocolate-coated,
        56, 80
    fruity, 80
Biscuits
    basic, 34–35
    buttermilk, 35

Blackberry pie, 173
Blondies
    basic, 58–59
    maple-walnut, 59
Blueberry
    muffins, 28–29
    pie, 172–173
Boston cream pie, 112–114
Boysenberry pie, 173
Bran muffins, 30–31
Breads
    cinnamon raisin swirl, 213
    cinnamon rolls, 233–235
    cloverleaf rolls, 222
    crescent rolls, 223
    dinner rolls, 221–223, 226
    equipment for making,
        199–201
    focaccia, 227–229
    French baguettes,
        224–226
    honey–whole
        wheat, 219
    kneading, 204–205
    pecan sticky rolls,
        230–232
    pizza dough, 236–237
    sourdough, 214–217
    storing, 209
    tips for making, 203–209
    white loaf, 211–213
    whole wheat loaf, 218–220

Brownies
    basic, 60–61
    chocolate chip cream
        cheese, 73
    cream cheese, 72–73
    peanut butter cup, 61
    peanut butter marbled, 73
Butter, use of, 4
Butter cookies, 62–63

C

Cakes
    angel food, 126–128
    Boston cream pie, 112–114
    carrot, 120–121
    cheesecake, 140–143
    chocolate angel food, 128
    chocolate chip
        cheesecake, 142
    chocolate chip layer, 123
    chocolate chip pound, 133
    chocolate–chocolate chip
        layer, 125
    chocolate layer, 124–125
    chocolate marbled
        cheesecake, 141
    chocolate marbled
        pound, 133
    coconut, 123
    coffee, 137–139
    decorating tips, 109–110

Cakes *continued*
  equipment for making,
    99–100
  frosting tips, 107–109
  German chocolate, 115–117
  lemon cheesecake, 142
  lemon–poppy seed, 118–119
  lemon pound, 133
  poppy seed pound, 133
  pound, 132–133
  pumpkin cheesecake, 142
  spice, 121
  sponge, 129–131
  storing, 110–111
  strawberry shortcake,
    134–136
  tips for making, 101–107
  yellow layer, 122–123
Carrot cake, 120–121
Cheesecake
  basic, 140–143
  chocolate chip, 142
  chocolate marbled, 141
  lemon, 142
  pumpkin, 142
  topping, 141
Cherry pie, 190–191
Chocolate
  angel food cake, 128
  biscotti, 55–57
  brownies, 60–61
  chip biscotti, 80
  chip blondies, 58–59
  chip cheesecake, 142
  chip coffee cake, 139
  chip cookies, 68–69
  chip cream cheese
    brownies, 73
  chip layer cake, 123
  chip macaroons, 75
  chip muffins, 46
  chip peanut butter
    cookies, 91

chip pound cake, 133
chocolate chip
  biscotti, 56
chocolate chip cookies,
  88–89
chocolate chip layer
  cake, 125
coated biscotti, 56, 80
cream cheese brownies,
  72–73
cream pie, 174–176
cupcakes, 125
decorations, 12–14
frosting, 146
German chocolate cake,
  115–117
glaze, 112–113
lace cookies, 82–83
layer cake, 124–125
marbled cheesecake, 141
marbled pound cake, 133
macaroons, 74
peanut butter cup
  brownies, 61
peanut butter
  frosting, 146
peanut butter marbled
  brownies, 73
pecan pie, 195
sponge cake, 131
toffee bars, 66–67
Cinnamon
  raisin bread, 213
  rolls, 233–235
Cobblers, fruit, 184–185
Coconut
  cake, 123
  cream pie, 182
  cupcakes, 123
  frosting, 145
  lemon bars, 85
  pecan frosting, 115–116
  toasting, 182

Coffee cake
  apple, 138
  basic, 137–139
  chocolate chip, 139
Cookies
  bar cookies, tips for, 51–52
  biscotti, 79–81
  blondies, 58–59
  brownies, 60–61
  butter, 62–63
  chocolate biscotti, 55–57
  chocolate chip, 68–69
  chocolate chip biscotti, 80
  chocolate chip
    macaroons, 75
  chocolate–chocolate
    chip, 88–89
  chocolate–chocolate chip
    biscotti, 56
  chocolate macaroons, 74
  cream cheese brownies,
    72–73
  crusts, 140–141, 162
  drop cookies, tips for, 49–50
  equipment for making,
    47–49
  fruity biscotti, 80
  gingerbread people, 76–78
  gingersnaps, 64–65
  lace, 82–83
  lemon bars, 84–85
  macadamia nut–white
    chocolate chip, 69
  macaroons, 74–75
  oatmeal raisin, 86–87
  peanut butter, 90–91
  peanut butter cup
    brownies, 61
  peanut butter marbled
    brownies, 73
  ranger granger, 70–71
  Rice Crispy marshmallow
    bars, 92–93

rolled cookies, tips for, 50–51
shortbread, 94–95
storing, 54
sugar Christmas, 96–98
tips for making, 52–54
toffee bars, 66–67
thumbprint, 63
Corn muffins, 44–45
Cranberry-orange bread, 36–37
Cream cheese
brownies, 72–73
frosting, 120–121
Crisps, fruit, 192–193
Crusts
cookie, 140–141, 162
pastry, 160–161
Cupcakes
chocolate, 125
chocolate chip, 123
chocolate–chocolate chip, 125
coconut, 123
yellow, 123

D

Date-nut bread, 20–21
Decorating
cakes, 109–110
pies, 153–156
plates, 10–11
suggestions, 10–12
with chocolate, 12–14
Dinner rolls
basic, 221–222
cloverleaf, 222
crescent, 223
crusty, 226

E

Egg whites, beating and folding,
103–105
Eggs, about, 4

Equipment
bread making, 199–201
cakes, 99–100
cookies, 47–49
general, 2
muffins and quick breads,
15–16
pies, 147–148

F

Flour
all-purpose, 3–4
bread, 3, 201
cake, 3, 100–101
whole wheat, 201
Focaccia, 227–229
French bread (baguettes),
224–226
Frosting and fillings
chocolate, 146
chocolate cherry, 146
chocolate glaze, 112–113
chocolate peanut butter, 146
coconut, 145
coconut-pecan, 115–116
coffee, 145
cream cheese, 120–121
custard filling, 112–114
hot fudge, 188–189
lemon, 144
lemon glaze, 118–119
mocha, 146
orange, 144
peanut butter, 144
tips for frosting layer cakes,
107–109
vanilla, 144

G

German chocolate cake,
115–117

Gingerbread people, 76–78
Gingersnaps, 64–65

H

Hot fudge sauce
basic, 188–189
flavored, 189

I

Ice cream
pie, 188–189
sandwiches, 69, 89
Icing, easy cookie, 76–78, 96–98

K

Key lime pie, 186–187

L

Lace cookies, 82–83
Lemon
bars, 84–85
cheesecake, 142
coconut bars, 85
frosting, 144
glaze, 118–119
meringue pie, 177–180
poppy seed cake, 118–119
poppy seed muffins, 22–23
pound cake, 133
tips for cooking with , 23,
85, 119, 179

M

Macaroons
basic, 74–75
chocolate, 74
chocolate chip, 75
Measuring ingredients, 7
Meringue topping, 177–180

Mocha
    frosting, 146
    pecan pie, 195
Mud pie, 188–189
Muffins
    banana-nut, 24–25
    blueberry, 28–29
    bran, 30–31
    chocolate chip, 46
    corn, 44–45
    equipment for making,
      15–16
    lemon–poppy seed, 22–23
    storing, 19
    streusel topping, 29
    tips for making, 17–19

O

Oatmeal raisin cookies,
    86–87
Oil, about, 4
Olallieberry pie, 173

P

Peach pie, 166–167
Peanut butter
    chocolate frosting, 146
    cookies, 90–91
    cup brownies, 61
    frosting, 144
    marbled brownies, 73
Pecan
    chocolate pie, 195
    mocha pie, 195
    pie, 194–195
    sticky rolls, 230–232
    sweet potato pie, 197
Pies
    apple, 163–165
    banana cream, 181–183
    blackberry, 173
    blueberry, 172–173

boysenberry, 173
cherry, 190–191
chocolate cream, 174–176
chocolate pecan, 195
coconut cream, 182
cookie crusts, 140–141, 162
cranberry apple, 164
decorating crusts, 153–156
Dutch apple, 164
equipment for making,
    147–148
French apple, 164
ice cream, 188–189
ginger-pecan topping, 169
Key lime, 186–187
lemon meringue,
    177–180
maple pumpkin, 169
mocha pecan, 195
mud, 188–189
olallieberry, 173
orange sweet potato, 197
pastry crusts, 160–161
peach, 166–167
pecan, 194–195
pecan sweet potato, 197
pumpkin, 168–169
raisin apple, 164
raspberry, 173
rolling pie dough,
    150–152
storing, 158–159
strawberry-rhubarb,
    170–171
streusel topping, 156, 164
sweet potato, 196–197
tips for making, 149–158
vanilla cream, 182
Pizza dough
    basic, 236–237
    herbed, 237
    whole wheat, 237
Popovers, 38–39

Pound cake
    basic, 132–133
    chocolate chip, 133
    chocolate marbled, 133
    lemon, 133
    poppy seed, 133
Pumpkin
    bread, 26–27
    cheesecake, 142
    maple pie, 169
    pie, 168–169

Q

Quick breads
    banana, 40–41
    cranberry-orange,
      36–37
    date-nut, 20–21
    pumpkin, 26–27
    storing, 19
    tips for making, 17–19
    zucchini, 42–43

R

Ranger granger cookies,
    70–71
Raspberry pie, 173
Rice Crispy marshmallow bars,
    92–93
Rolls
    cinnamon, 233–235
    cloverleaf, 222
    crescent, 223
    crusty, 226
    dinner rolls, 221–223
    pecan sticky, 230–232

S

Scones
    basic, 32–33

double raisin, 33
fruity, 33
Shortbread
basic, 94–95
butter pecan, 95
lemon–poppy seed, 95
Sourdough bread,
214–217
Sponge cake, 129–131
Sticky rolls, 230–232
Strawberry-rhubarb pie,
170–171
Strawberry shortcake,
134–136
Sugar Christmas cookies,
96–98
Sugar, types of, 4
Sweet potato pie
basic, 196–197

pecan, 197
orange, 197

T

Toffee bars, 66–67

V

Vanilla
cream pie, 182
frosting, 144

W

Whipped cream
flavored, 189
for banana cream pie, 181
for chocolate cream pie, 174

for Key lime pie, 186
for mud pie, 188
for strawberry shortcake, 134
tips for making, 189
White loaf bread,
211–213
Whole wheat bread
basic, 218–220
honey, 219
seedy, 219

Y

Yeast, 5, 201–202
Yellow layer cake, 122–123

Z

Zucchini bread, 42–43